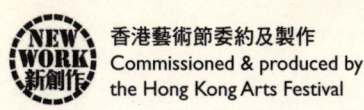

香港藝術節委約及製作
Commissioned & produced by
the Hong Kong Arts Festival

《聖荷西謀殺案》
Murder in San José

莊梅岩 Chong Mui-ngam

英文翻譯 張敏儀
English Translation Margaret Cheung

翻譯改編 黃哲倫
Translation Adaptation David Henry Hwang

New Plays Selection books by:

www.musemag.hk

Foreword

There is a view that words on a page are like orphans, with no one to give them articulation and no defense against possible misreading.

This is not the intended fate of words written for the stage. They are meant to be framed in a carefully controlled environment, spoken skillfully by talented actors who have painstakingly prepared the delivery of every syllable for a receptive audience to achieve maximum effect.

While the words on the following pages will not truly come alive until these conditions are satisfied, I hope their potential is evident, even when stripped and orphaned on the page, awaiting your imagination – or the resources of a full production – to animate them.

This is the third year in which the Festival has commissioned, produced and published new works. The intention is not only a matter of record, but also to facilitate each work's progress from the first Festival production to other stagings and re-imaginings, as a resource to the artistic community in Hong Kong and elsewhere in the world. Even while celebrating the premiere, I look forward eagerly to future productions.

It is a great pleasure and privilege to be able to present these words to you. I am grateful to my talented and dedicated colleagues for making it possible. I would also like to thank the many artists who work with us to bring the Hong Kong Arts Festival to life each year.

Tisa Ho
Executive Director, Hong Kong Arts Festival

前言

有一種說法認為，紙上的文字就像孤兒，既無人解讀，亦無人為其可能引起的誤讀辯護。

舞台劇本卻不應落得如此命運，它們應享有一個如溫室般的理想環境，由具才華的演員經過多番經營，才向一群有心的觀眾宣之於口，以達到最佳效果。

在未有這些條件以前，這本書中的文字仍沒有完整的生命，但我希望讀者能感受到這些紙上孤兒的潛質，它們正等待你的想像力，或者製作資源來賦予它們生命力。

這是藝術節委約、製作和出版新劇作的第三年，我們的目的不單是作為一份紀錄，更希望這次的首演能為香港以至世界各地的藝術社群帶來更多的重演和改篇劇目。在慶祝首演之際，我更期待未來的演出。

能在這裡與您分享以上的話，我深感榮幸。感謝各位能幹又勤奮的同事，令這個計劃得以實現。我亦要向所有藝術家說聲謝謝，全賴你們的參與，才能成就每一年的香港藝術節。

何嘉坤
香港藝術節行政總監

playwright's notes

Just as I was about to write this prologue, a Hollywood film playing on television caught my eye. It was about a character in a novel. When he sensed that the plot decreed his eventual death, he tried everything he could to make the author revise the manuscript. His predicament struck a chord with me as I too experienced the same dilemma as a playwright. There was indeed a time when I felt a character I created was asking me in a wounded tone:

"Do I really have to die?"

"What if I reformed and became a better person?"

"Would you let me live on?"

The only difference was the response I chose – silence. I let the days go by, embracing new people and things in order to remove the memory of that lament.

Each time my play is staged, I am confronted by a pair of searching eyes. I really want to tell her that when a playwright hardens his heart to bump off a character, it is not to flaunt his authority, or for the sake of achieving closure in his work. Sometimes, death provokes questioning, and questions bring opportunities.

This play is dedicated to those who have forgotten about existence.

莊梅岩
Chong Mui-ngam

CHONG MUI-NGAM graduated from Royal Holloway, University of London with a Master's Degree in Playwriting. She also holds Bachelor's Degree in Psychology from The Chinese University of Hong Kong and an Advanced Diploma in Playwriting from The Hong Kong Academy for Performing Arts.

Chong has translated *The Shape of Things*, *Betrayal* and *Flowers for Algernon*. She has received Best Script Awards at the Hong Kong Drama Awards for her plays *Alive in the Mortuary*, *Shall We Go to Mars?*

and *The French Kiss*. In 2003, she was awarded the Outstanding Young Playwright Award by the Hong Kong Federation of Drama Societies, and in 2004 the Asian Cultural Council presented her with the Lee Hysan Foundation Fellowship, which enabled her to spend one year studying in the US.

She received the Best Script Award for the fourth time for her play *Murder in San José*. Her translation of *Chinglish* was shown in Chicago in June 2010 and her first original opera debuted in Beijing in September 2010.

編劇的話

正要為此下筆，看見電視播放著某荷里活影片，講述一個角色如何意識到自己將被推向死亡而千方百計尋找小說家，請求她不要讓自己在故事中死去。無獨有偶，筆下角色也曾懷著同樣受創的心靈問我：

「不可以不死嗎？」

「如果我會變得更好呢？」

「不能繼續生存嗎？」

不同的是，我以沈默回應，讓時日過去，用新的人和事，去忘卻那個失落的靈魂。

今天，戲要上演了，再度面對那雙垂詢的眼神，我很想告訴他，一個劇作者狠下心腸去謀殺一個角色，未必為了炫耀權力，未必為了成就寫作。有時候，讓死亡帶來叩問，叩問本身就是一種契機。

獻給 遺忘了存在的人們

香港中文大學社會科學院心理學榮譽學士、香港演藝學院戲劇學院編劇系深造文憑畢業。英國倫敦大學Royal Holloway編劇碩士。

除撰寫舞台劇外，亦參與劇本翻譯，包括《改造情人》、《背叛》、《天才一瞬》等。憑《留守太平間》、《找個人和我上火星》及《法吻》獲第12、14及15屆香港舞台劇獎最佳劇本獎；2003年獲香港戲劇協會頒發傑出青年編劇獎；2004年獲亞洲文化協會頒發利希慎獎學金赴美遊學一年。

2010年憑《聖荷西謀殺案》第四度獲得最佳劇本獎。翻譯作品《Chinglish》於2010年6月在芝加哥演出，首個原創歌劇於2010年9月在北京首演。

導演 Director

李鎮洲 Lee Chun-chow

編劇 Playwright

莊梅岩 Chong Mui-ngam

主演 Cast

劉雅麗 Alice Lau 飾演 玲 Ling

鄧偉傑 Tang Wai-kit 飾演 Tang

彭秀慧 Kearen Pang 飾演 Sammy

張䢂米 Jimmy Zhang 飾演 Ming

梁小衛 Priscilla Leung 飾演 Zoë

葉 進 Yip Chun 飾演 Patrick

舞台及服裝設計 Set & Costume Designer
曾文通 Tsang Man-tung

燈光設計 Lighting Designer
劉銘鏗 Lau Ming-hang

音樂 Music & Sound Designer
Frankie Ho

製作經理 Production Manager
張向明 Cheung Heung-ming

執行監製 Executive Producer
陳志勇 Andrew Chan

監製 Producer
香港藝術節 The Hong Kong Arts Festival

首演 PREMIERE
第37屆香港藝術節 at the 37th Hong Kong Arts Festival
第一次重演於2009年8月27 - 31日, 9月2 - 6日
1st Re-run from 27 - 31 August and 2 - 6 September 2009

第二次重演於2011年3月3 - 13日
2nd Re-run from 3 - 13 March 2011

國際巡演 INTERNATIONAL TOUR
新加坡濱海藝術中心劇院2011年4月1 - 2 日
1 - 2 April 2011, Esplanade Theatre, Singapore

角色簡介 Characters

玲： 三十八歲，在美國半工讀
下完成大學課程，畢業後便下嫁
Tang，選擇留美定居

LING: 38. A college graduate
through part time studies in the US..
She married Tang after graduation
and chose to stay in America.

TANG： 四十六歲，正籌備發展
自己的生意。與Ling相識於大學
時代。

46. He is preparing to start his own
business. He met Ling during college.

SAMMY： 三十五歲，演唱會舞蹈
員，變賣半生積蓄到美國旅行，最
後一站來到聖荷西，探訪自小敬愛
有加的兒時鄰里Ling。

35. A pop concert dancer. She used
half her life savings to vacation in
America. Her last stop is San José to
visit Ling, her childhood neighbor
whom she idolizes.

PATRICK： 五十多歲，大陸人，
鄧氏夫婦來往得比較多的中國
人。

50s. A Mainland Chinese. The most
closely connected Chinese with the
Tangs.

ZOË： 四十多歲，大陸人，Patrick
的妻子。

40s. A mainland Chinese. Patrick's
wife.

明哥： 四十二歲，台灣人，Ling
舊同事。

MING: 42. Taiwanese. Ling's former
colleague.

序幕

聖荷西一華人家庭的獨立大屋。

觀眾進場前幕已開啟：一個晴朗的早上，女主人站在大門旁的窗前，似乎正等待什麼人的到來。陽光鉤勒出她的背影，同時進駐到她身後的客廳、飯廳和開放式廚房，到處窗明几淨，顯示她勤快而又井井有條。

隨著時間的流逝男主人開始在屋內走動，都是一些自然和合乎生活的舉動。他讓我們感到有一條走廊連接睡房和儲物房，另有一條樓梯引上二樓。除了大門，這幢房屋尚有兩個出口，一個通往車房，一個通向花園。事實上他幾次進出花園，想要作些園藝卻又因慵懶而放下。最後索性從冰箱裡拿出預先弄好的沙律來吃。

夫婦倆沒有交談，除了男人走動時發出的聲響，就剩下遠處傳來的「拍拍」聲，像一扇未關好的木門，只有在畫面靜止時才顯得突兀。整個家就這樣沐浴在悠閒與寧靜之中。

觀眾就坐完畢，台燈漸暗，慢慢現出橫亙在地板之下那個被重重綑綁的人。虛弱地用身體發出最後幾聲納悶的求救訊號

燈再暗，序幕完 。

PROLOGUE

A standalone home of a Chinese family in San José.

The curtain is open as the audience enters the theatre. It is a sunny morning. The female owner of the house stands at the window by the main entrance as if she is waiting for someone. The light etches her silhouette and projects it into the living room and the open kitchen behind her. It is clean and tidy everywhere, indicating she is an efficient and organized homemaker.

As time passes, the male owner of the house enters and moves about, in a manner indicative of ordinary life. He gives us the feeling that there is a hallway that connects to the bedroom and storage room. There is a staircase leading to the second floor. Apart from the main entrance, there are two more exits, one leading to the garage and the other to the garden. In fact, he enters and exits to the garden several times. He seems to want to garden but gives up due to laziness. Eventually, he retrieves a prepared salad from the refrigerator and eats it.

The husband and wife do not talk. Apart from the noise that the man makes as he moves, there is just a banging noise from afar, as if a door has not been shut properly. The noise is most prominent when the stage is still. The couple bathes in leisure and stillness.

When the audience is seated, the house light dims and slowly reveals a tied-up individual beneath the floorboards, who feebly uses the few last ounces of energy to send out a confused cry for help.

Fade out. End of prologue.

第一場

【*電話鈴聲響徹黑夜。良久，走廊燈亮，一孕婦步出接聽電話*】

玲： ……Hello?……你去咗邊？我哋喺屋企等咗你成日呀……你唔好講住，你依家喺邊？到咗San José未吖？……應該到咗？咩叫應該到咗？……係吖……係嘞……【*一邊聽一邊走到樓梯向上呼叫*】Tang！Tang……冇嘢，我叫阿Tang出去接你，你繼續講我聽緊——你繼續講啦！你話出咗101跟住點話？……Stanford、Palo Alto、係吖，喺Portola Valley轉入Old La Honda Road，跟住條路咪一直上山囉……係，係咁架，條路係彎彎曲曲，D樹老練咁粗架嘛……【*一男子睡眼惺忪從樓梯下*】咁你過咗個木林未——佢出咗個木林喇，你出去——荒廢咗嘅餐廳？冇理由，呢度方圓30里都唔會有餐廳。

TANG： Rosie Diner，佢落咗舊區。

玲： 你點會行咗去嗰邊，我咪叫你出木林之後靠左行，過咗山頂個草地一落斜就到，零零舍舍得一間冇可能認錯！

TANG： 講咩都冇用，佢行錯咗。

玲： 你叫開車嗰個同我講，你哋行錯路，仲越嚟越遠。

TANG： 唔係太差啫，原路返嚟應該唔使五分鐘——

<u>SCENE 1</u>

(A telephone rings in the middle of the night. A while later, the hallway lights turn on. A pregnant woman enters to answer the telephone.)

LING ... Hello? ... Where have you been? We waited for you all day... Hold it. Where are you right now? Are you in San José yet? ... You should be? What do you mean "should"? ... Yes... Yes... (*As she talks on the telephone, she shouts towards upstairs.*) Tang! Tang! ... Nothing, I'm just calling Tang to go meet you. Keep talking, I'm listening. OK, you exited 101, and then what? Stanford, Palo Alto, yes, turned into Old La Honda Road at Portola Valley, then just followed the road up the hill... Yes, that's right. The road is very windy, lots of really thick tree trunks, right? (*A sleepy man descends from upstairs.*) So have you left the woods? (*to the man*) She's left the woods. Go outside. ... (*to the phone*) An abandoned restaurant? That can't be right. The closest restaurant from here is, like, 30 miles.

TANG Rosie's Diner. She's in old town.

LING How did you end up there? I told you to stay on the left when you got out of the woods. Go past the field on top of the hill and keep going down. There's only one house. You can't miss it.

TANG Forget it. She took the wrong turn.

LING Let me talk to the driver. You're on the wrong road. Going in the wrong direction.

TANG It's not so bad. Just make a U-turn. It shouldn't take them more than five minutes to get here.

玲： 梗係唔得啦！嗰條係單程路，依家黑媽媽，佢反方向行上嚟萬一有車衝落山點算——你聽住，千祈唔好諗住兜返原路上嚟，咁樣好危險架！張詠兒呀，你唔想客死異鄉就聽我講！

【*玲一邊已把地圖展開*】

TANG： 你唔係想教佢喺Palo Alto轉個圈先上返嚟嘛。咁有排搞喎，萬一佢哋再行錯——

【*玲已埋首地圖*】你叫佢落唐人街食埋宵夜至上嚟喇 / 我上去瞓先。

玲： 喂？ / 你正話同邊個講英文？你唔係話Las Vegas有香港人上三藩市順便車埋你咩？你同香港人都講英文？仲要係帶墨西哥口音嘅香港男人——你唔好話俾我知你搭緊順風車！

【*將電話筒遞給Tang，逕自走開*】

TANG： 俾我做咩啫？

玲： 俾佢激死。

TANG： ……喂……我係阿Ling個老公……我諗佢依家唔係咁得閒，佢忙住幻想你點俾D公路殺手肢解呀、姦屍呀咁……

玲： 我覺得一D都唔好笑。地圖。

TANG： 你有冇紙筆？阿Ling想我講條路線你知——佢有地圖喎——話時話你可以就到先再打過嚟，咁我哋可以閂多一陣嘛……哦……

玲： 你叫佢落返101跟住La Honda個水牌。

TANG： OK……唔緊要——

LING   Are you insane? It's a one-way street. And dark out there! They drive against traffic, they'll hit someone coming up the hill. Listen, do not make a U-turn! That's very dangerous. Cheung Wing Yee, you wanna die overseas? Then listen to me! (*Ling has opened up a map.*)

TANG   You're not going to make her go all the way back to Palo Alto, are you? That would take forever. What if they get lost again? (*Ling is at the map.*) Tell them they might as well get a snack in Chinatown before they turn around. I'm going back to bed.

LING   Hey! Who were you speaking English to? You said you were getting a ride from Las Vegas with some Hong Kong people! So why are you speaking English? I hear a Mexican accent! Oh my god, don't tell me you hitched a ride! (*Hands the telephone to Tang. She moves away.*)

TANG   What?

LING   She's driving me crazy.

TANG   … Hello? This is Ling's husband… I think she's a little busy right now, imagining you being slaughtered and raped by highway murderers…

LING   That's not funny. The map.

TANG   Do you have a pen? Ling wants me to give you directions. She's got her map. Listen, call us again when you get closer, ok? That way we can sleep a little longer… Oh…

LING   Tell them to get back on 101 and follow the signs to La Honda.

TANG   OK… No problem…

玲：　　　點啫，你識唔識講啫？

TANG：　　冇問題。唔好咁講。晏D見。Bye。

玲：　　　你做乜唔教清楚佢點行呀？

TANG：　　人哋都話有地圖，個墨西哥佬識點行㗎喇。

玲：　　　識行頭先又行錯？

TANG：　　人哋冇你咁叻，睇錯地圖囉。

玲：　　　所以你咪應該講一次俾佢聽囉。嘖！仲要冇來電顯示。

【稍頓】

TANG：　　……還搰起咗身……我諗你個friend都鍾意飲酒。

玲：　　　呢個張詠兒，成日做嘢都係咁不顧後果……美國一年有幾多公路兇殺案，喺條街打個手勢就有免費車搭？俾人溶咗都唔知咩事，仲要一個單身女仔，佢真係唔知驚。

TANG：　　冇事嘅，都嚟到門口。

玲：　　　你又知？話唔埋個墨西哥佬見我哋住得偏僻，綁起晒我哋三個將間屋洗劫一空呢？呢D唔係飛來橫禍？電視都有得睇，就上個月之嘛，喺downtown有家人俾兩個後生仔持械行劫，入屋第一件事喺工人身上開一槍然後指住五歲個細路嘅雲精：「如果唔想冇咗佢兩分鐘之內將所有值錢嘢攞出嚟」——依家D人發起窮惡，手唔震汗都有一滴，你敢同佢搏？……你即管笑，好多受害人遇害之前都好似你咁笑……鬼唔望個墨西哥佬一入嚟就打爆你枝85年Mouton。

LING	What? Did you hear me?
TANG	No problem. Don't worry. See you later. Bye.
LING	Why didn't you give them the directions?
TANG	They said they have a map. That Mexican guy knows the way.
LING	Then how come he got lost?
TANG	He's not as smart as you. He read the map wrong, OK?
LING	You should have given him the directions again. No caller ID. (*Slight pause.*)
TANG	Now that we're up... I guess your friend would like a drink.
LING	That girl, she's so disorganized... There're millions of highway murders in the US every year, she could've hitched a ride with anyone. If she disappears, no one will even know. A single girl? What an idiot.
TANG	They're almost here. She'll be fine.
LING	What do you know? What if that Mexican sees that our place is really remote and he can just tie the three of us up and rob us blind? There's no such thing as coincidence. You see it everyday on TV. Just last month, a family downtown was robbed by two armed youths. Entered the house and shot the maid, just like that. Then they pointed the gun at the son – a five-year-old kid! – and said, "If you don't want to lose him too, hand over all your valuables in two minutes." Poor people these days have no qualms. They shoot without batting an eye. You can't fight them. Fine, laugh. A lot of victims laughed just like you before they got robbed... I hope the first thing that Mexican shoots is your '85 Château Mouton.

TANG: 你有冇毒D呀？

玲: 所以呢，損失呢D嘢好難預計⋯⋯其實屋企真係應該買返把槍。

TANG: 枝tequila用完。

玲: 新嗰枝喺雪櫃左手邊櫃頂⋯⋯我都估到，先前喺Las Vegas打過嚟都古古怪怪，我問佢班香港人個車牌號碼啦，萬一有咩意外都追得返吖嘛，一陣話唔記得問一陣話問咗唔記得，原來，班人駕車同個車牌根本冇存在過⋯⋯唔怪得知依家先到，慌唔係截咗成日先截到呢架咩──我又唔明，真係會有人立亂俾個陌生人跳上車，佢哋唔怕呢個係局嚟架咩？

TANG: D司機唔係立亂俾人上車嘅。

玲: 咪就見佢係弱質女流囉，一個孭住大背囊，貌似嚟旅行嘅弱質女流。我梗知張詠兒唔會老笠個司機，但係如果有班壞人夾埋，派個女仔出去搭順風車然後引D司機返嚟劏死牛，個墨西哥佬係咪好危險呢？既然截同被截嗰個都咁大風險⋯⋯為乜呢？真係好難理解⋯⋯話時話聽日交換車用。

TANG: 點解呀？

玲: 我架車冇咁食油，聽日你載佢周圍去揸我架車冇咁嘥油。

TANG: 咩呀？！

玲: 信我啦，你架野馬次次落downtown兜個圈就冇咗半缸油。

TANG: 揸你架車冇所謂，但係我載佢周圍去？

TANG   You're evil.

LING   All I'm saying is that you should think about what you could lose. Maybe we should get a gun.

TANG   The tequila is finished.

LING   There's another bottle in the cupboard… I knew it. She sounded funny when she called from Vegas. I asked her for the license plate of the Hong Kong guy's car, in case anything happens. One moment, she says she forgot to ask, the next moment, she said she forgot after she asked. The driver, the license plate – never existed. No wonder she's so late. I bet it took her all day to hitch a ride. I don't get it. Why would these drivers pick up a total stranger? Aren't they worried it might be a trap?

TANG   They don't pick up just anyone.

LING   Well, they can see she's a young girl. They see her toting a backpack and know she's a travelling, feeble, young girl. Of course Wing Yee wouldn't rob the driver, but some rowdies could use her as bait, then, when a driver pulls over, jump out and rob him! That Mexican is in danger too! Both the driver and the hitchhiker risk so much. Why? I just don't get it. Speaking of which, trade cars with me tomorrow.

TANG   OK. Why?

LING   My car gets better mileage. You take her around tomorrow. Drive my car, it's more economical.

TANG   What?

LING   Trust me. Your Mustang is a gas-guzzler. One trip downtown, and the tank is half empty.

TANG   I'm ok with driving your car, but – you want me to take her around?

玲： 係呀，咁我要返工吖嘛。

TANG: 你唔係請咗假陪佢咩？

玲： 今日咋，我諗住佢第一日到吖嘛，點知佢咁晏先至到，嘥咗我一日假——

TANG: 幫你唔到，我聽日有嘢做。

玲： 有咩做呀？

TANG: 網上超市嗰單嘢囉，我之前有同你講過。

玲： 哦，去傾嘢。

TANG: 係呀，一早約好咗架。

玲： 唔可以改第二日咩？

TANG: 唔得。

玲： 你都未試。

TANG: 唔得呀！人哋好忙架！你又係嘅，明明聽見你話會請一個禮拜假陪佢，依家好似旨意晒我咁嘅？

玲： 我諗住連埋D產假先一次過放吖嘛，而且Heather啱啱走咗，個個做到踢晒腳……一係咁，我請星期五，你約星期五。

TANG: 咩星期五唧？你以為我約人出嚟傾吓計飲吓咖啡呀？我去「哀」人出錢俾我做生意呀，仲要人哋改時間表嚟就我！不如我直接打去同佢講「老細，我有心搞起呢壇嘢架，不過我老婆個姊妹嚟咗，我要陪佢去完遊山玩水先讀個計劃書你聽呀！」咁呀？

玲： 有朋自遠方來，佢明嘅。

LING	Yeah. I have to work.
TANG	Didn't you get the day off?
LING	Just today. I thought she'd arrive during the day. Who knew she'd be this late? I totally wasted my day off.
TANG	I can't. I got work to do tomorrow.
LING	What work?
TANG	The online emporium. I told you.
LING	Oh, the meeting.
TANG	Yeah, I made the appointment a while back.
LING	Can't you change it?
TANG	No.
LING	You haven't even tried.
TANG	I can't. They're very busy. I thought you said you took a week off to be with her. Now you want me to take care of her?
LING	I decided to save my days for maternity leave. Besides, Heather just left. Everyone is pushed to the max. All right, I'll get Friday off. Move your appointment to Friday.
TANG	What do you mean Friday? You think this is a date for coffee? I am going there to beg people for money for my business. You want them to change the appointment to please me? Maybe I should just call them and say, "Dude, I'm serious about the business, but my wife's friend is in town. Lemme take her around, then I'll show you my proposal."
LING	She came a long way. They'll understand.

TANG:	你係咪痴線架？！你以為我真係會咁同佢講？人哋仲肯同我做生意嘅──你成日都係咁，你嘅事先係事，我嘅事唔係事嚟嘅！我都未話你，呢頭叫我唔好請人上嚟坐，轉個頭自己就叫人嚟住！咁都算，嗰個張咩咩係你朋友嚟架嘛，點解你講到照顧佢係我嘅責任啫？！
玲：	冷靜D。

佢叫張詠兒。如果你真係唔想照顧佢，我唔會迫你。不過我想你諗吓，兩夫妻，我嘅朋友如果只係我嘅朋友，咁你嘅阿媽係咪只係你嘅阿媽？咁即係下個月我可以唔寄生活費俾佢？

【*稍頓*】

順便分清楚呢間屋邊樣嘢屬於邊個人連個B都切開一半哩？

TANG:	成個俾晒你，我都冇話過要。
玲：	嘷，你又嚟，我都講咗，好多決定係冇得返轉頭，我哋只可以用一種正面D嘅心態面對佢。

張詠兒係個舊朋友，原本都唔諗住覆佢，不過我後來諗，自從搬過嚟新屋我哋就好似斷晒六親，都唔係咁好，依家難得有個朋友可以聚吓舊，都唔錯吖……你都識講，我哋幾何有朋友上嚟？你唔係打算喺我哋嘅客人面前表露呢種不滿嘛？

【*靜場，Tang在玲跟前放下兩杯雞尾酒*】

傻咗呀你？

TANG:	另外嗰杯唔係俾你。
玲：	你咁早整定，佢嚟到咪暖晒囉？

TANG   Are you crazy? You think they'd do business with me if I said that? You always do this to me. Your job is everything, my job is nothing. I'm just getting started here. You ask me not to invite anyone home. Then you turn around and invite your friend to stay. Fine. But this Cheung something-or-other is your friend. And now I end up taking care of her?

LING   Calm down. Her name is Cheung Wing Yee. If you don't want to take care of her, I'm not gonna force you. I just want you to think about it. We're married. If my friends are only my friends, then is your mother only your mother? Does that mean I don't have to pay her living expenses next month? (*Slight pause.*) If you want to divide everything in the house, should we divide the baby too?

TANG   You can keep the baby. I never said I wanted it.

LING   There you go again. I told you. Some decisions can't be reversed. We have to face this with a positive attitude. Cheung Wing Yee is an old friend. I wasn't even going to reply to her. But then I thought, it's like we've shut ourselves off from the world since we moved here. That can't be good. And since she was visiting, I thought it would be nice to spend time with a friend. That's not so bad, is it? Like you said, we never have visitors. You're not going to be all cranky in front of our guest, are you? (*Silence. Tang places two cocktails in front of Ling.*) Are you crazy?

TANG   The second one's not for you.

LING   By the time she gets here, it won't be cold anymore.

TANG:　　Ling，唔係樣樣嘢都一定照你安排架。

【*屋外傳來汽車響按聲*】

【*Tang慢慢披上外套，玲則快步走到窗前眺望*】

玲：　　你一早知佢原路上嚟？你一早都唔喝住佢？【*看一看手錶*】仲要開到咁快──出去叫佢唔好再響按！一陣人哋以為我哋呢度發生咩事──喂！唔好請個墨西哥佬入嚟，記住抄低佢車牌……

【*Tang從大門離開，玲仍佇足眺望*】

……噴！一睇就知係咸濕佬……

……嘩，仲要咁肥……

【*玲進房，屋外傳來清脆女聲：「Adios! Gracias! Mucho gracias!......」由遠至近，「得……等我嚟，唔該晒……嘩！好勁呀，Hou屎呀！我有Friend住Hou屎呀──嘩！咩嚟架──唔好住，去搵崔巧玲先！」*】

SAMMY:　　鄧師奶！喂！【*大門開，Sammy上，背上手裡都提著包包，Tang手提另外兩件行李尾隨*】嘩……我覺得好似入咗西片呀！痴線架，兩個人使唔使住咁大呀？仲有二樓添！總共有幾間房呀？嘩，個廚房好大呀……個雪櫃都好大──仲有吧枱……係呀係呀！我覺得屋企係要咁鬥出嚟至有home feel！你諗吓聖誕嘅時候外面落住雪，窗邊有棵聖誕樹閃吓閃吓咁──咩嚟架──！Shit！唔係嘛，我喺屋企擺棵文竹都嫌阻掟你哋有個──花園……離晒譜……你笑咩？

TANG   Ling, not everything can be the way you want it. (*A car horn sounds. Tang slowly puts on his coat. Ling quickly goes to the window.*)

LING   You knew she made a U-turn and you didn't tell me? (*Looks at watch.*) They must have raced all the way here. Go out and tell him to stop honking. People will think there's a problem. And don't invite the Mexican in. And get his license plate number... (*Tang exits through main entrance. Ling watches.*) ...He looks like a creep ... Oh my god, he's so fat. (*Ling enters the bedroom. A young woman's voice is heard from outside the house "Adios! Gracias. Muchas gracias..." Her voice approaches "I got it... Thanks... Wow... Beautiful... A whole house! My friend lives in a house. Wow... What's that? Oh wait, let me find Chui Hau Ling first."*)

SAMMY   Mrs. Tang? Hello? (*The main entrance door opens. Sammy enters. She is carrying bags on her back and in her hands. Tang enters behind with two pieces of luggage.*) Wow... I feel like I just walked into a Hollywood movie. This is insane. Two people living in such a huge house. And a second floor! How many rooms? Wow... the kitchen is huge. The refrigerator is huge...and the dining room table... This wood is gorgeous. Yeah! The engraving makes me feel right at home. Just imagine the snow outside during Christmas, a blinking Christmas tree by the window... What's this? Shit! Jesus, I can't even have a potted plant at home and you have a...whole garden? This is ridiculous... What are you laughing at?

TANG: 加州冇雪落。

SAMMY: 【笑】暴露咗我嘅無知添。大肚婆呢？唔係咁
快瞓返嘛？

TANG: 頭先都喺度……

SAMMY: 喂！鄧師奶！鄧師奶──

【玲手拿外套出】

玲： 喺度呀叫到咁大聲──搞咩呀？一袋二袋咁
嘅？好心你出門就帶大D嘅喼喇……Tang，車
房好似有兩個吉喼，聽日剷出嚟俾佢裝嘢返香
港，還揾用唔著……做咩唧？凍就摟住，咪抵
冷貪蕭湘。

SAMMY: ……崔巧玲。

玲： 點呀張詠兒。

【Sammy擁抱玲，良久，玲感到她在啜泣。微
笑】

唔使咁煽情嘛。

SAMMY: 乞人憎！想對你好D都唔得……

【Sammy放開玲，接過外套】

我冇諗過你大肚係咁……

玲： 未介紹呵，我老公，鄧少昌；香港D朋友，張詠
兒。

SAMMY: 鄧生吖嘛！叫我Sammy得喇，都未恭喜你添，
第一次做Daddy心情一定好興奮哩？

玲： 叫佢阿Tang得喇，呢度D鬼都係咁叫佢。

SAMMY: 文明D啦鬼鬼聲！香港都立咗法你移民過嚟咁耐
都唔改唔到口。

TANG	It doesn't snow in California.
SAMMY	(*Laughs*) I just gave away my ignorance, didn't I? Where is the mother-to-be? Don't tell me she's gone to bed.
TANG	She was just here…
SAMMY	Hey, Mrs. Tang. Mrs. Tang… (*Ling enters with a coat.*)
LING	I'm here. Don't shout. What's with all the bags? Why didn't you bring a larger suitcase? Tang, I think there are a couple of empty suitcases in the garage. Haul them out and let her take them back to Hong Kong. They're just sitting there. What? Put this on. Don't catch a cold just so you can look good.
SAMMY	…Chui Hau Ling!
LING	How are you, Cheung Wing Yee? (*Sammy and Ling hug for a while. Sammy is close to tears. She smiles.*) You are so melodramatic.
SAMMY	Damn it. Just want to be nice to you. (*Sammy releases Ling. Takes coat.*) I didn't think you'd look like this pregnant.
LING	My husband Tang Siu Cheong. Cheung Wing Yee, my friend from Hong Kong.
SAMMY	Mr. Tang. Call me Sammy. I forgot to congratulate you. First-time daddy. You must be excited.
LING	Just call him Tang. All the gweilos here call him that.
SAMMY	Be civilized, will you? Hong Kong has passed a law. And you've lived here so many years. Can't you be more politically correct?

玲：　　　　咁係因為香港D鬼佬識聽你哋至唔叫，稱呼嚟啫，夠冇人叫我做chink咯代唔代表呢度冇種族歧視吖。

SAMMY：　　【熱情地擁著玲】係你喇！崔巧玲係咁架！

玲：　　　　過嚟坐，阿Tang整咗杯嘢歡迎你。

SAMMY：　　嘩Margarita！我最鍾意Margarita——

玲：　　　　喂係咪應該解釋吓車你上嚟嗰班香港人點解突然消失呢？

SAMMY：　　咪咁啦，我冇錢呀。

玲：　　　　唔信。

SAMMY：　　呢你做乜嘢，我喺New York洗大咗呀！你哋呢到又tax又tips，D錢好似倒水咁倒，後尾我已經盡慳架喇，點知去Arizona嗰程機計漏機場稅，白白唔見幾舊水，到Las Vegas身上得返廿蚊美金，心諗：還掂都唔夠搭shuttle bus，未賭返舖囉，卒之，財散人安樂——係個實Q教我去油站睇吓有冇人順路上三藩市，佢話嗰頭D司機見慣嘅……

玲：　　　　打個電話上嚟吖嘛，幫你訂張車飛冇幾難啫？

LING　　　The only reason you can't say it in Hong Kong is because the gweilos there can understand it. It's just a word. Nobody calls me chink, but that doesn't mean racism doesn't exist here.

SAMMY　　(*Hugs Ling passionately.*) That's the Chui Hau Ling I know.

LING　　　Come, sit here. Tang fixed a cocktail to welcome you.

SAMMY　　Wow, a margarita! My favourite.

LING　　　Hey, how come those Hong Kong people you were supposed to ride with seem to have disappeared?

SAMMY　　Give me a break. I ran out of money.

LING　　　Yeah, right.

SAMMY　　Why would I lie? I spent too much in New York. You got all these taxes and tips here. The money slipped through my fingers. I tried to spend less but forgot I had to pay airport tax for the flight to Arizona. I lost a few hundred dollars there. When I arrived in Las Vegas, I only had US$20 cash. And I thought, since I don't have enough for the shuttle bus, I might as well gamble. Finally, once I lost everything, I stopped. It was the security guard who told me about getting a ride to San Francisco at the gas station. He said drivers are used to it.

LING　　　You should've called us. We could've bought you a bus ticket.

SAMMY: 我諗住截唔到就向你求救㗎喇，竟然俾我遇到Mario！佢真係super Mario，超好人！趕住送貨落San Diego都車我上嚟先，仲請我食熱狗——哎呀，頭先掛住搵路唔記得問佢攞e-mail添……anyway，佢趕時間咋，唔係實入嚟同你say hi，我同佢講我個好朋友就嚟生BB，佢仲話Oh, I have to kiss the mum's belly……

TANG: 係就好，我都想睇吓阿Ling點一腳伸佢返墨西哥。

【*Sammy 笑，Tang在玲身邊坐下*】

玲: 佢係咁，一有外人喺度就懶幽默。

【*舉起水杯*】循例都要講句：當呢度自己屋企。【*玲看一看Tang*】

TANG: 係囉，阿Ling嘅朋友即係我嘅朋友。

【*Sammy又想落淚，玲給她一個眼色*】

SAMMY: ……我唔客氣喇。【*三人碰杯*】

玲: 點呀，諗咗去邊度玩未呀？

TANG: 人哋啱啱至到埗俾佢抖啖氣先好冇？

玲: 好晏喇，依家講定啱㗎喇。

TANG: 可能人哋聽日想留喺屋企呢？

玲: 點會啫，香港人時間就係金錢。

SAMMY: 唔係呀，我真係想留喺屋企，玩咗成個月咩都玩夠，係時候偷窺吓你哋嘅家庭生活。

玲: 無嘢嘛，山長水遠嚟過家庭生活？

SAMMY   I would've called you if I couldn't hitch a ride, but I met Mario. He is so nice. He was supposed to make a delivery to San Diego, but he detoured to drive me here first. He even treated me to a hot dog… Oh no, I forgot to get his email… Oh well, he was in a hurry, otherwise, he would've come in to say hi. I told him you're about to give birth and he said, "Oh I have to kiss Mama's belly".

TANG   I would've loved to have seen Ling kick him back to Mexico. (*Sammy laughs. Tang sits next to Ling.*)

LING   He's always such a smart-ass around strangers. (Lifts glass.) I should still say, as is the custom, make yourself at home. (*Ling looks at Tang.*)

TANG   Absolutely. Ling's friends are my friends. (*Sammy is near tears again. Ling gives her a look.*)

SAMMY   Then I'll make myself comfortable. (*They clink glasses.*)

LING   So? Do you know where you want to go?

TANG   She just got here. Let her rest first.

LING   It's late. She can rest after we decide.

TANG   Maybe she just wants to stay home tomorrow.

LING   She won't. To Hong Kong people, time is money.

SAMMY   No, I do want to stay home tomorrow. I've been travelling for a whole month; it's time for me to share your family life.

LING   Are you kidding? You came all the way here for family life?

SAMMY: 冇所謂架，個重點係探你！而且你哋有自己嘅做，唔好俾我破壞你哋嘅生活規律，得架喇，由我自己喺屋企hea得喇。

TANG: 我鍾意你呢個朋友，佢好體貼。

玲： 係啫，一場嚟到冇理由淨係喺喺度，至少都去吓漁人碼頭、金門橋咁啦？你唔知有咩玩咋？西岸D風景好靚，《斷背山》咪喺度拍架囉，我寄俾你D旅遊資料你有冇睇過？

SAMMY: 咩旅遊資料？

玲： 上個月你一話過嚟我就去旅遊局撢咗D介紹書寄俾你，仲特登用FedEx添！

SAMMY: 哎呀，打俾你嗰陣我已經搬咗。

玲： 咁架你，搬屋都唔講聲嘅？

SAMMY: 我冇諗過就嚟見面你都會寄嘢俾我架嘛——死喇，冇人收退返嚟會唔會charge多你一次架？

玲： 噴……你搬返去同你家姐住呀？

SAMMY: 唔係，租開嗰度業主加租，咪求祈搵間房租住先囉。

玲： 你失戀呀？

SAMMY: 咩呀，都話業主加租，咪失戀啫，好耐冇戀過啦。

玲： 你唔係有個做警察嘅男朋友咩？

SAMMY: 嗰個係我第一份暑期工識，散咗N年啦！

SAMMY   It's all right. I came here to visit you. And you have to work. I don't want to mess up your routine. I'll be fine. Just let me hang out in your home.

TANG   I like your friend. She's very considerate.

LING   Still, you can't just sit here. You at least have to go and see Fisherman's Wharf and the Golden Gate Bridge. You just don't know the sights, right? The views out West are beautiful. *Brokeback Mountain* was shot here. Where's all that sightseeing information I sent? Did you read it?

SAMMY   What information?

LING   Soon as I heard you were coming last month, I went to the tourism office and got a bunch of brochures. I even couriered them to you.

SAMMY   I'd already moved when I called you.

LING   Why didn't you tell me you'd moved?

SAMMY   I didn't think you'd send me all that stuff. I just wanted to come here and see you. Oh no, will you have to pay a penalty if no one accepts it?

LING   Did you move back to your sister's?

SAMMY   No, my landlord raised the rent so I just found a room and moved there for a while.

LING   You broke up with someone?

SAMMY   What?! I told you, my landlord raised my rent. I didn't break up with anyone. I haven't dated anyone for a while.

LING   Weren't you dating a policeman?

SAMMY   Yeah, during my first summer job. A century ago!

TANG: 喂，你哋究竟係咪識架？

玲： 點知佢，D男朋友好似走馬燈咁轉。

SAMMY: 唔好聽崔巧玲講，佢走咗之後乜都唔知架佢
——我以前喺Dance School有個拍咗好耐架。

玲： 你仲做緊dancer呀？

SAMMY: 係呀，不過返去可能轉工，你知啦，跳咗咁多
年都攰，返去想試吓第二D嘢——

玲： 話咗你啦，呢行邊做得長——

SAMMY: 得得得得！我完全feel到你想講乜——識整
cocktail都唔灌醉佢，成世人都咁清醒。

TANG: 佢係咁，我諗要搵碌棍兜頭「牛」落去佢至唔
清醒……【Sammy 笑】

咁呢個月你實去咗好多地方，去Arizona有冇上
大峽谷呀？聽講好靚架喎。

SAMMY: 靚架！我幾奢侈，坐直昇機兜咗個圈！不過抵
架，一望無際，grand到呢——你哋喺美國咁
耐都冇去過咩？

TANG: 佢話遲D等BB識性至全家一齊去喎。

玲： 咁係吖嘛，嗰D地方去一次就夠，還掂都要去，
等多五年，五年。

SAMMY: 崔巧玲呀，有D嘢係要襯後生做架，我哋已經
miss咗好多。你知唔知，我喺Grand Canyon
就見到四個中國女仔喺度映相，其中一個——
喺大峽谷面前裸體。

TANG   Do you two really know each other?

LING   Who can keep track? She's always got a new boyfriend.

SAMMY   Don't listen to Ling. She knows nothing about me anymore. When I was still at Dance School, I dated someone for a long time.

LING   Are you still dancing?

SAMMY   Yes, but not for long. You know how it is. After all these years dancing, I'm tired. When I go back, I want to try something else.

LING   I told you. You can't dance forever…

SAMMY   Yadda, yadda, yadda! I know what you're gonna say. (*To Tang*) You're so good at making cocktails, you should make her one. She's too uptight.

TANG   I know. I have to hit her over the head to knock her out. (*Sammy laughs.*) You must've seen a lot of sights on your travels. Did you go to the Grand Canyon when you were in Arizona? I hear it's beautiful.

SAMMY   Yes, totally. I went all out. I took a helicopter tour, but it was worth it. Sky as far as the eye can see. It was awesome…You've never been there? You've lived here so many years.

TANG   She said we should go later – as a family, when the baby is older.

LING   Well, sure. You only have to see it once. If we want to go, we can wait five years.

SAMMY   Chui Hau Ling, there are some things we should do while we're young. We've missed a lot already. You know, at the Grand Canyon, I saw four Chinese girls taking photos. One of them was naked.

TANG: 嘩，咪好壯觀？

SAMMY: 壯觀架！為國爭光呀。

玲： 做咩唧，你想映咩？

SAMMY: 如果有個信得過嘅人揸機，我制架。

玲： 你幾時變得咁開放架？

SAMMY: 有幾開放呀！

TANG: 有幾開放呀？

SAMMY: 咪係！留個紀念之嘛──哎，俾D相你哋睇。

【一邊從背包拿出照相機】

TANG: 好──

玲： 好咩呀，唔好喺我屋企發佈淫褻及不雅照片吓。

SAMMY: 我話旅行D相呀！

玲： 話時話，唔好映我相呀，費時你一陣放喺嗰D咩facebook呀blog咁，全世界都見到。

SAMMY: 鬼得閒upload你D相上網──應承你，就算映咗我都淨係私人珍藏。咁多年冇見，你結婚嗰餐我又冇份飲，依家大住肚，我好想映低你個幸福樣，唔係第時老咗淨係記得你個忟忟蹭蹭樣……

【Sammy為二人拍照，將照相機遞給Tang】

吖，估唔到你有睇我個blog吓。

玲： 開頭咋，仲好講，寫埋D嘢咁無聊。

TANG   Wow, must've been quite a sight.

SAMMY   Yes. Made me feel proud to be Chinese.

LING   What? You wanna take photographs like that?

SAMMY   If I could trust the photographer, sure, I would do it.

LING   When did you become so liberated?

SAMMY   That's not liberated.

TANG   It's not?

SAMMY   No. It'd just be a souvenir. Here, let me show you my photos. (*Takes out photos from knapsack.*)

TANG   Oh good…

LING   Good? Don't you dare bring out pornographic pictures in my home.

SAMMY   I meant my sightseeing photos.

LING   By the way, don't take my photo. I don't want you to post my photos on your blog or Facebook for the whole world to see.

SAMMY   I have better things to do than upload photos of you. I promise. I will only take photos of you for my personal collection. It's been so many years. I didn't get a chance to go to your wedding. Now that you're pregnant, I want a record of your happy life. Otherwise, when I'm old, I'll only remember your mean face. (*Sammy takes their photos then hands Tang the camera.*) Hey, I didn't know you read my blog.

LING   Just the beginning. You write such nonsense.

SAMMY:	係咩……我都好耐冇寫。【*Tang和玲繼續看照片，Sammy看著他們，靜場*】
玲：	咩呀？
SAMMY:	……冇呀。
玲：	……冇？你有D唔妥喎。
SAMMY:	呢個月頻頻撲撲有D劫之嘛，真係冇嘢呀！
玲：	唔係嘅……直接D啦係咪想問我借錢呀？
SAMMY:	痴線架……哈哈哈……你講咗去邊呀？！我冇嘢呀，我只不過諗起以前D嘢，細個成日上你屋企玩……呢，老豆送我返學，去到斜坡底就會由我跟你行……後來升上中學，我又成日去你做Part Time間7仔食思樂冰……
玲：	……根住呢？
SAMMY:	根住咩？
玲：	你想講咩唧？
SAMMY:	冇，我係話，時間過得真係快……依家你有自己嘅屋企，好快又有自己嘅小朋友……我好戥你開心……
玲：	有咩開心唔開心吖，都係咁過架啦。
TANG:	你唔係最想俾人睇到你幾幸福咩？依家又講埋D咁嘅嘢。Sammy，D相映得好靚。

SAMMY   Well, I haven't written in a long time. (*Tang continues to take Ling's photo. Sammy watches them. Quiet.*)

LING   What's the matter?

SAMMY   Nothing.

LING   Something's wrong.

SAMMY   I'm just a little tired from all the running around lately. I'm fine.

LING   No… Be straight with me. You want to borrow money?

SAMMY   No, I don't – ! What are you talking about? I'm fine. I was just thinking about how I used to go to your house to play. When my father would take me to school, he'd let me go with you from the bottom of the hill. Then, when I was in high school, I would always go to that 7-11 where you worked and buy ice cream.

LING   What about it?

SAMMY   What about what?

LING   What are you trying to say?

SAMMY   Nothing. It's just that time passes quickly. Now you have your own home and soon you'll have children. I'm just happy for you.

LING   Nothing special about that. It's life.

TANG   What are you saying? I thought you wanted to show her your happy married life. Sammy, take a nice photo for us.

玲： 咁係吖嘛，依家睇梗好架，我哋啱啱喺Chicago搬過嚟嗰陣，幾哩hea呀，個屋頂漏水，花園又種極都唔生，我記得頭嗰兩個月周圍見工，一返嚟就同阿Tang哩屋企整呢整路，幾劫⋯⋯不過係幾開心嘅，Tang呵？

TANG： 係。

玲： 你都著緊D，有仔趁嫩生，細我嗰幾年，就嚟到你做高齡產婦。

SAMMY： 即刻搵件結婚然後一擊即中或者可能趕得切嘅⋯⋯係喎，趁我呢幾日喺度，有咩好貨唔怕介紹──一於咁話，唔使帶我去咩景點，帶我去相睇，金山阿伯都殺，呢期我最想搵個人嫁咗去。

玲： 玩咩，睇中點算？

SAMMY： 咪stay喺度囉，你都係咁啦。

玲： 你捨得你家姐至算啦。

SAMMY： 佢搬咗入愉景灣啦，我依家見佢嘅次數同移咗民差唔多⋯⋯OK呀OK呀！真係諗得過！你諗吓如果住埋喺附近，咁我哋咪有伴囉！

玲： 好喎，咁我留返D BB衫俾你。

TANG： 呢D叫做十劃都未開始磨墨。

SAMMY： 磨定嗮架喇，好開心呀──陀仔係咪好辛苦架／我可唔可以掂吓呀？／我淨係想摸咋唔係想襟呀／好得人驚呀／咁襟法會唔會俾咁D嘢出嚟架⋯⋯

LING   It's true. Things look good now. But when we moved here from Chicago, they were a mess. The roof leaked and everything in the garden died. The first two months, all I did was look for a job. Every night after I came home, Tang and I would be working on one thing or another. We were exhausted. But we were happy. Right, Tang?

TANG   Yup.

LING   If you want children, have them when you're still young. You're only a few years younger than me. Soon, you'll be old – with a "mature pregnancy". You need to be more farsighted.

SAMMY   You're right, I'd better find someone, marry, and get knocked up immediately! But … I'll be here for the next few days if you wanna set me up. It's settled. You don't need to take me sightseeing. Just arrange a match for me. Rich old men will do fine. I am ready to get married.

LING   Very funny. What if you like the guy?

SAMMY   Then I'll stay here. Like you did.

LING   You couldn't leave your sister.

SAMMY   She moved to Discovery Bay. I hardly see her anymore. But you have to admit, it's a good plan. If I lived around here, we'd have each other.

LING   Sure, you can have my second-hand baby clothes.

TANG   That's really premature.

SAMMY   It's not so premature. This is fun. Is it hard to be pregnant? / Can I touch it? / I just want to touch, not press. / That's amazing. / If I squeeze here, will something come out?

玲： 　有幾辛苦吖，個個都係咁陀架啦／咪揣囉／唔怕，大力D啦／係咪呀淋D呀／呢邊係Pat Pat呢邊咪手手腳腳囉⋯⋯

TANG： 　⋯⋯你哋慢慢摸，我瞓先⋯⋯

玲： 　喂，幫張詠兒攞咁D嘢落地牢先——你唔使樣樣跟身，唔用嗰D阿Tang幫你攞落去，唔使阻住D地方⋯⋯

SAMMY： 好呀。

　　　　　【*Tang正要動身整理行李*】

玲： 　咁聽日你——

TANG： 　咩呀，Sammy都話要留喺屋企⋯⋯咪俾佢留喺度囉。

玲： 　咁阿Tang留喺屋企陪你，順便整嘢俾你食。

TANG： 　喂——

SAMMY： 唔使唔使！真係唔使——不如你試吓我手勢啦，呢幾日喺度白食白住，俾我貢獻吓。

玲： 　一於咁話，你煮俾佢食。

　　　　　【*稍頓*】

　　　　　咩呀。

TANG： 　冇，我好鍾意你咁安排。

　　　　　【*Tang默默走向行李堆*】

玲： 　咁你聽日休息吓，weekend我哋就落漁人碼頭睇日落⋯⋯

SAMMY： 你話事啦⋯⋯靠你喇Tang，我唔敢去咩地牢，睇鬼片多數呢D位出事⋯⋯

LING　　What's hard about it? All women go through the same thing. / Go ahead and touch. / Don't worry. You can press harder. / This is softer, right? / This side is the tush and the arms and legs are over here…

TANG　　…You guys keep chatting. I'm off to bed…

LING　　Hey, take Sammy's bags to the basement. You don't need everything with you, right? What you don't need, Tang will take downstairs.

SAMMY　　OK. (*Tang is about to move luggage.*)

LING　　So tomorrow you…

TANG　　Sammy said she wants to stay home. Let her.

LING　　Then you stay home with her, Tang. Cook for her.

TANG　　Um …

SAMMY　　You don't need to do that. Really. Why don't you try my cooking? I'll be living off you. Let me contribute.

LING　　Fine. You can cook for him. (*Slight pause.*) What?

TANG　　Nothing. I love your arrangement. (*Tang walks silently to the luggage.*)

LING　　You rest tomorrow. We'll go to Fisherman's Wharf this weekend and watch the sun set.

SAMMY　　You decide. Thanks, Tang. I don't want to go to the basement. That's where all the creepy things lurk in scary movies.

玲： 　　　你咪咁無聊啦，我哋買之前check得好清楚，呢間屋好乾淨架。【*Sammy神色奇怪*】你唔使嚇我張詠兒，我唔會俾你玩到。

SAMMY： 　　……唔係哩……

玲： 　　　做咩呀？

SAMMY： 　　……好似……少咗一件。

玲： 　　　唔係嘛。

SAMMY： 　　……我有個細細地、粉紅色嘅唸……

　　　　　　【*三人面面相覷*】

TANG： 　　　……可能漏咗喺外面，我出去睇吓！

　　　　　　【*Tang外出，Sammy翻行李*】

玲： 　　　你會唔會套咗喺嗰個唸入面？有冇擸上車架？會唔會漏咗喺酒店？

SAMMY： 　　唔會架，我全程都放喺大脾……我……死喇，點會咁嘅……

　　　　　　【*Tang折返*】

玲： 　　　冇呀？

　　　　　　【*Tang搖搖頭*】

　　　　　　豈有此理！等我打911捉咗個死人墨西哥佬！車牌？

TANG： 　　　……頭先太多嘢拎，無手抄低。

LING	Don't be ridiculous. We checked the place out before we bought it. This house is clean. (*Sammy's reaction is strange.*) Don't try to scare me. I'm not that gullible.
SAMMY	No, it's just …
LING	What?
SAMMY	I think… I'm missing something.
LING	You're kidding.
SAMMY	I had a small pink suitcase… (*They eye each other.*)
TANG	Maybe it's still outside. I'll go look. (*Tang goes outside. Sammy searches her luggage.*)
LING	Is it in one of the other bags? Did you bring it in the car? Did you leave it at the hotel?
SAMMY	No, I had it on my lap in the car. I… Oh no… How could I… (*Tang returns without success.*)
LING	Anything? (*Tang shakes his head.*) Damn it! Call 911 and report that spic driver. What's his plate number?
TANG	…I was carrying so much luggage, I forgot to write it down.
LING	What are we going to do? Tell the police some fat Mexican has stolen a pink suitcase? I told you. Nobody is that nice. Coming to San José was way out of his way. I told you to take down the plate number. Every time I tell you to be careful, you think I'm nagging.
TANG	…Yes, you can predict the future.

玲： ……咁點呀？唔通我同個警察講有個墨西哥肥佬偷咗佢個唸呀？我都話，邊有咁大隻蛤蟆隨街跳，去San Diego條路一D都唔經San José，所以呢，我先叫你抄低車牌，每次叫你小心D都當我發噏風……

TANG： ……係呀你最料事如神你係先知。

SAMMY： 傻啦邊關佢事吖！一日都係我！我自己唔小心，我太容易信人——不過各位，佢真係白抬喇，因為成個唸都係D無謂嘢……你知我幾鍾意買無謂嘢啦，都係D好平嘅souvenir，有個音樂盒我幾鍾意咁囉，不過冇咗都冇所謂。

玲： 係？

SAMMY： 嗯！

玲： 是但……咁擺D嘢落去啦。【*Tang靜靜地搬行李*】

SAMMY： 唔該晒你呀Tang，唔該晒，真係唔該晒……

【*Tang下樓*】

玲： 噴……死人墨西哥佬！

SAMMY： ……可能頭先太趕喇，Mario擺漏咗。

【*稍頓*】

玲： 張詠兒，咪咁天真啦。【*稍頓*】坐吓，我入去擺對拖鞋俾你……【*玲走了幾步復折返*】呀係——我哋呢度都冇乜嘢，係唔好喺屋裡面食煙。阿Tang有氣管敏感，同埋……

SAMMY： 我發誓，我一定唔會喺你間屋食煙——我本身都諗住戒架喇。

SAMMY   It's not his fault. It's mine. I was careless. I'm too trusting. But it won't do him any good. There's nothing valuable in that suitcase. You know how I like to collect junk. It's just cheap souvenirs. There's a music box I kinda liked, but it doesn't matter.

LING   You telling the truth?

SAMMY   Yes.

LING   Whatever... Then take the rest downstairs. (*Tang quietly takes the luggage.*)

SAMMY   Thanks so much, Tang. Really, thanks a lot... (*Tang goes upstairs.*)

LING   Goddamn Mexican.

SAMMY   Maybe we were in too much of a rush and he left my bag in the car. (*Slight pause.*)

LING   Sammy, don't be so naïve. (*Slight pause.*) Sit here. I'll get you some slippers. (*Ling takes a few steps and returns.*) Oh yeah, we don't have any house rules, just no smoking indoors. Tang has allergies. Also...

SAMMY   I would never smoke in your house, I swear. I was thinking of quitting anyway.

玲： 咁又唔使發誓咁嚴重……不過戒咗都好，食煙對皮膚唔好，尤其你未生BB，生子宮癌嘅機會已經高……

【*Sammy目送玲離去，想到自己的煙味，在掌心呵了口氣，惘然地坐在這偌大的客廳，燈滅*】

LING   You don't have to swear, but quitting is good. Smoking is so bad for your skin, especially when you haven't had children. You're at high risk for cervical cancer. (*Sammy watches Ling exit. She thinks about her tobacco stench and breathes into her palm. She sits in the big living room, lost in thought. Lights fade out.*)

第二場

【*清晨，家裡播放著懷舊廣東歌，Tang從二樓下來，見四處無人，花園門卻開著，正要走向花園，Sammy從正門入*】

TANG: 咦？

SAMMY: 早晨！

TANG: 早晨。

SAMMY: 冇，我見郵差派信，咪出去幫你哋攞囉。

TANG: 攞信都咁開心嘅……唔該。

【*Tang接過信件便放在一邊*】

SAMMY: 你唔拆開嚟睇？

TANG: 唔慌有信寄俾我。

SAMMY: 唔係呀，呢封咪係囉。

TANG: 哦，網上繳費D嘢，阿Ling會搞。係呢點解……

SAMMY: 崔巧玲留咗張字條叫你除草……幾日架喇，我見還掂起咗身——

【*Tang正想走出去*】

唔使緊張——我知有D係佢特登種落去，佢要你扷嘅係呢D吖嘛……

【*Sammy將膠筒遞向Tang*】

TANG: 阿Ling好緊張個花園，我費事佢一陣又呱呱嘈。

SAMMY: 【*笑*】我明嗝。

SCENE 2

(*Morning. Classic Cantonese pop songs are being played. Tang enters from upstairs. He sees that the living room is empty but the door to the garden is open. As he approaches the garden, Sammy enters from the front door.*)

TANG   Oh!

SAMMY   Morning, Tang.

TANG   Morning.

SAMMY   I saw the postman so I thought I'd get the mail for you.

TANG   Getting the mail seems to put you in a good mood ... Thanks. (*Tang takes the mail and puts it down.*)

SAMMY   Aren't you going to open them?

TANG   They won't be for me.

SAMMY   No, this one here is for you.

TANG   Oh, it's just online payment stuff. Ling will take care of that. By the way, why are you ...

SAMMY   Ling left a note from a few days ago telling you to weed the garden. I was up early so I thought I'd... (*Tang wants to go outside.*) Don't worry. I know what was planted on purpose. She wanted you to pull these. (*Sammy hands Tang a plastic pail.*)

TANG   Ling is very fussy about the garden. I just don't want her to get upset.

SAMMY   (*Laughs*) I understand.

TANG: ……尤其係D玫瑰花，佢搞咗好耐先種到出嚟——

SAMMY: 寧寧舍舍有欄圍住嗰D吖嘛，放心，我冇掂。

【稍頓】

我整早餐俾你食。

TANG: 你唔瞓多陣？尋晚同阿Ling傾到好夜哩？我見好晏個廳都著住燈。

SAMMY: 崔巧玲囉，把口話瞓喇瞓喇，自己又猛start話題，我冇所謂，驚佢今日返工冇精神——佢幾癲，今朝起身見到佢畫俾我張家居平面圖，佢將D咖啡呀、嘢食呀嗰D位置列晒出嚟——

TANG: 仲有CD。

SAMMY: 仲有CD囉——

TANG: 佢係咁，自己覺得係寶就係咁塞俾人。

SAMMY: 我都覺得好sweet，不過唔知佢畫到幾點，你知啦，大肚婆應該休息多D架嘛。

TANG: 放心啦，佢有嘢嘅，你要睇佢剪完樹枝喺條梯跳落嚟個樣，我覺得佢就嚟可以幫自己接生。

SAMMY: 哈……邊有可能啫……坐嗰邊吖，幫你set咗個位。

TANG: 哦。搵唔到咩開聲喎。

TANG   …Especially the roses. It took her a long time before she got them to bloom.

SAMMY   They have fences around them, right? Don't worry. I didn't touch them. (*Slight pause.*) C'mon. I'll fix you breakfast.

TANG   Why didn't you get more sleep? You and Ling must've talked – I saw the lights on until really late.

SAMMY   It was Chui Hau Ling's fault. She kept saying she had to go to bed, then she just kept talking. It doesn't matter to me, but she had to go to work this morning. She's crazy. This morning I saw the floor plan of the house she drew for me. She labelled the locations of the coffee and the food.

TANG   And the CDs.

SAMMY   And the CDs.

TANG   That's Ling. Whatever she thinks is important, she pushes onto you.

SAMMY   I think it's sweet. Now that she's pregnant, she ought to rest more. I wonder when she went to bed last night.

TANG   Don't worry. She's fine. You should see the way she jumps off the ladder after she prunes the trees. That woman will deliver her own baby.

SAMMY   (*Laughs*)…Don't be silly. Sit there… I set a place for you.

TANG   Oh. If you need anything, just let me know.

SAMMY:	OK。【*靜場，Sammy開始準備早點，Tang無所事事，不時看電話*】
SAMMY:	要唔要咖啡呀？
TANG:	好呀。
SAMMY:	⋯⋯煎蛋定scramble eggs？
TANG:	Scramble eggs吖。【*稍頓*】 唔該。
SAMMY:	——
TANG:	咩呀？
SAMMY:	Dejavu。
TANG:	咩dejavu？
SAMMY:	我好似喺邊度見過咁。
TANG:	見過咩？
SAMMY:	你未試過咩，即係有時你去到一個新嘅地方或者見到一D新嘅人，你明知到冇可能見過都有種似曾相識嘅感覺⋯⋯
TANG:	即係好似D人話：小姐，我好似喺邊度見過你。
SAMMY:	唔係呀⋯⋯唔知呢，總之我啱啱問你食煎蛋定scramble eggs，你答scramble eggs吖，唔該，呢吓唔知喺邊度見過咁。
TANG:	哦——咁如果我答煎蛋呢？
SAMMY:	哈⋯⋯咁就冇lu。
TANG:	你都唔似香港女仔嘅。

SAMMY   OK. (*Silence. Sammy begins to prepare breakfast. Tang has nothing to do and constantly looks at his mobile phone.*) Want some coffee?

TANG   Sure.

SAMMY   Fried or scrambled?

TANG   Scrambled. (*Slight pause.*) Thanks. What?

SAMMY   Déjà vu.

TANG   What déjà vu?

SAMMY   I've seen this somewhere else.

TANG   Seen what?

SAMMY   Hasn't it ever happened to you? Like, when you go to a new place or meet someone for the first time? You know you've never seen them before but you get this familiar feeling.

TANG   Like, when someone says, "Hey, babe, haven't we met somewhere before?"

SAMMY   No…I don't know. It's just that, when I asked you fried or scrambled, and you said "Scrambled. Thanks." I felt like I'd seen this before.

TANG   Oh. What if I'd said fried?

SAMMY   Then it wouldn't be déjà vu.

TANG   You're not like other Hong Kong girls.

SAMMY: 點解咁講呀？

TANG: 香港女仔應該會話：哈……爛gag。

SAMMY: 你又知，你都冇返香港你又知依家香港D女仔變成點？

TANG: 港女吖嘛，呢個大名連維基百科都有，依家有咩係上網查唔到。所以我都知道，頭先你只係大腦其中一邊處理訊息嘅速度稍稍快過另一邊。

SAMMY: 咩呀？你話dejavu？

TANG: 嗯，我上網查過。

SAMMY: 真架？

TANG: 所以下次有男仔同你講：小姐，我好似喺邊度見過你，你就可以答——唔使驚，咁係由於你大腦其中一邊處理訊息嘅速度稍稍快過另一邊啫。

SAMMY: 唔該晒，你啱啱用科學殺死晒所有嘅浪漫。

TANG: 已婚嘅男士就係咁㗎。

SAMMY: 亂噏。我見過D已婚男士不知幾浪漫。

TANG: 咁嗰D想昆你上床啫。

SAMMY: 哈——

【頓】

OK。

TANG: 嗯。

SAMMY: OK。我冇講嘢。

SAMMY Why do you say that?

TANG A 'HK girl' would've said, "What a lame joke."

SAMMY How do you know? You haven't been back to Hong Kong. How do you know what 'HK girls' are like now?

TANG 'HK girl'? It's on Wikipedia. You can find everything on the web. That's why I know that what you experienced just now is the result of one side of your brain processing information at a slightly higher speed than the other side.

SAMMY What? You mean déjà vu?

TANG Yeah. I looked it up.

SAMMY Really?

TANG So the next time a guy says to you, "Hey, babe, haven't we met somewhere before?" You can say, "Don't worry. That's only because one side of your brain is processing information at a slightly higher speed than the other side".

SAMMY Thanks. You just used science to kill romance.

TANG That's what married men do.

SAMMY Nonsense. I've met some very romantic married men.

TANG Yeah, the ones that want to sleep with you.

SAMMY Ha! (*Pause.*) OK.

TANG Uh huh.

SAMMY OK. I didn't say anything.

TANG: 我都冇問。

【一陣沈默的微笑】

SAMMY: 聽崔巧玲講，你都幾浪漫喎。

TANG: 我係OK架。

SAMMY: 聽講你哋喺pub識。

TANG: 係吖，我哋響酒吧識。

SAMMY: 估唔到，崔巧玲以前都唔飲酒嘅。

TANG: 人會變嘅。

SAMMY: 咁又係。

TANG: ⋯⋯尤其去到外地，你知啦，人生路不熟，佢朋友又唔多。嗰陣佢成日自己一個人落pub⋯⋯喺Chicago，落住大雪天寒地凍都揸車落嚟，開頭我仲以為佢想追我。

SAMMY: ⋯⋯唔係你追佢架咩？哦，大家講嘅版本開始唔同喇⋯⋯

TANG: 我話開頭啫。係，係我追佢嘅。我見佢成日嚟，以為佢鍾意我，仲懶風趣咁走埋去獻身，當然，俾佢使出港女嘅看家本領寸到我頭耷耷⋯⋯

SAMMY: 所以你就整咗杯崔巧玲特飲。

TANG: 咩嚟架？

SAMMY: 佢話你較咗杯cocktail以佢命名嘛，仲唔係叫崔巧玲特飲？

TANG: 嘩⋯⋯你呢D就真係叫做殺死浪漫，你搞到阿Ling好似變咗杯利賓納咁。

TANG   I didn't ask you anything. (*A silent smile.*)

SAMMY   Ling tells me you're very romantic.

TANG   I'm not too shabby.

SAMMY   I heard you met at a bar.

TANG   That's right. We met at a bar.

SAMMY   I never would've guessed. Ling never even used to drink.

TANG   People change.

SAMMY   That's true.

TANG   …Especially when they go somewhere else. You can imagine how it was. She was in a strange place with only a few friends. She used to go to the bar by herself… In Chicago, she'd drive there even when it was snowing hard. At first, I thought she wanted to make a move on me.

SAMMY   …I thought it was you who made the move on her. Uh oh, your versions conflict …

TANG   I said at first. True, I was the one who actually made the first move. I thought she liked me because she was at the bar all the time. So I waltzed up and generously offered myself. Of course, she gave me the cold shoulder….

SAMMY   That's why you created a Ling's Special?

TANG   A what?

SAMMY   She said you created a cocktail in her honour. A Ling's Special.

TANG   Now… that's what I call killing romance. You make Ling sound like a glass of Ribena.

SAMMY: 我唔知呀，咁佢冇話我知杯cocktail叫咩名嘛。

TANG: ⋯⋯視乎情況啦，睇吓阿Ling飲，Fanny飲定Tammy飲——不過！不過——依家齋叫太太特飲。

SAMMY: 算你啦。

TANG: 你話有乜辦法唔死，俾老婆「目及」住都算，仲要派個姊妹嚟「目及」。

SAMMY: 你再嘈我爆俾崔巧玲知你用同一杯cocktail追幾條女。

TANG: 都唔算嘅，亞玲佢鍾意Lime，我有係咁二加多D⋯⋯佢又鍾意用goblet杯，間pub冇架，我零零仃仃買咗係一隻⋯⋯都算係為佢整嘅。佢一開始唔睬我架，仲有一排冇落嚟，係我搵上門，日日著到成隻粽咁企喺巴士站等佢。

SAMMY: 終於就俾你打動⋯⋯你真係勁⋯⋯講樣嘢俾你知吖，其實我從來都冇諗過崔巧玲會結婚，佢亞爸亞媽喺我哋以前住個屋邨有個花名，叫靚聲孖寶，因為佢哋一嗌起交上嚟個成個天井嘅人都會閂埋門⋯⋯嗰陣崔世伯周不時攞晒D錢去賭，搞到崔伯母成日要加班，於是乎崔巧玲就要獨力照顧四個細佬妹，讀中學嘅時候佢已經成日同我講，如果有得俾佢揀，佢寧願自己一個人⋯⋯但係佢依家成個人變晒，又叫我積極D搵男朋友，又話咩有仔趁嫩生⋯⋯尋晚佢講起你嗰個樣⋯⋯我從未見過佢咁嘅，我直情覺得佢願意為你放棄晒所有嘅嘢。

【*Tang微笑不語*】一個女人願意為你咁樣改變，你一定有D嘢。

SAMMY   I don't know. She didn't tell me the name of the drink.

TANG   That depends on who's drinking it: Ling or Fanny or Tammy. But! But for now, it's called My Wife's Special.

SAMMY   That's better.

TANG   I am so screwed! Watched, not only by my wife, but by her friends too!

SAMMY   Watch it, or I'll tell Ling you used the same drink to make passes at other girls!

TANG   That's not exactly true. She said she liked limes, so I added a bit more. She said she liked using goblets. We didn't have any in the bar so I bought one for her. So, in a way, I guess the drink was created for her. At first, she wouldn't pay any attention to me. Then she disappeared for a while. I went to look for her near her home. Every night, I bundled up to wait for her at the bus stop.

SAMMY   And you finally got to her. You're amazing. Let me tell you something. I actually never thought Ling would get married. Her parents had a nickname in the complex where we lived. They were known as the couple with the golden voices, because when they fought, the whole place would shut their doors. Her father gambled a lot. Her mother had to work extra hours. Ling had to take care of four brothers and sisters. She always used to say to me in high school, if she had a choice, she'd rather be alone. But now she's completely changed. She tells me seriously to find a boyfriend and that I should have babies while I'm still young. Last night, when she spoke about you…I've never seen her like that before. I just feel like she would give up everything for you. (*Tang smiles.*) You must be very special if a woman is willing to do that for you.

TANG: 唔知呢，我同阿Ling……我哋幾乎係一拍即合、一嚓即著……但係又冇一閃即逝，所以就喺埋咗一齊……我諗女人其實可以好簡單：佢唔開心嗰陣靜靜地留喺佢身邊就得。

【一陣沈默】

SAMMY: 又係維基教你架？

TANG: 人生閱歷嚟嘅。

SAMMY: 扮晒嘢【笑】你有幾多歲呀？

TANG: 我？【稍頓】過埋生日四十七。

SAMMY: 四十七？你四十七？真係唔似喎！

TANG: 唔恨得咁多，到咗某個階段我哋個生理時鐘睇起上嚟係行得慢D。

【Sammy行近，要把他看得仔細】

喂，你唔好好似發現深山童老咁啦。

【略將Tang的眼鏡向下移，二人四目交投】

SAMMY: 你唔帶眼鏡個樣仲細呀！

TANG: 你唔好再晒太陽，D雀斑出晒嚟喇。

SAMMY: 我先唔驚，嗰D我trade mark嚟架。

【Sammy 將Tang的眼鏡托回原處，退開】

TANG: 都話你唔似香港女仔啦。

SAMMY: ……真係唔公平。我以為你大我幾年咋，原來你已經四十七。

TANG: 嗱，咁講嘢就冇晒氣質，應該咩年紀都對自己有信心。

| TANG | I don't know. Me and Ling... We were almost an instant pair. Sparks flew right away. The sparks continued so we stayed together. I think women are pretty simple When she's upset, I just sit quietly by her side. (*A moment of silence.*) |

SAMMY — Did you get that from Wikipedia too?

TANG — From life.

SAMMY — Come on, you're not so old. How old can you be?!

TANG — Me? (*Slight pause.*) Forty-seven on my next birthday.

SAMMY — No way! Are you kidding? You're 47? You are 47? You don't look it.

TANG — No need to envy me. At a certain point in life, time starts to run a little slower for guys. (*Sammy approaches him to take a closer look.*) Hey, don't act like you just saw the Creature from the Black Lagoon, OK? (*Lowers Tang's glasses. They make eye contact.*)

SAMMY — You look even younger without glasses.

TANG — Stop tanning. You're getting freckles.

SAMMY — I'm not worried. That's my trademark. (*Sammy puts Tang's glasses back and backs away.*)

TANG — I told you, you're not like other Hong Kong girls.

SAMMY — That's not fair. I thought you were just a few years older than me. But you're in your 40s.

TANG — Now that's not a very impressive thing to say. You should feel confident at any age.

SAMMY:	咁係吖嘛，有乜可能你可以keep得咁好架……
TANG:	係又點啫，無用武之地架。
SAMMY:	你唔使喺我面前講埋D咁嘅嘢，我唔信有男人專一，雖然我都祝福崔巧玲。
TANG:	唔係專唔專一嘅問題，係同階段。男人唔係成世都諗住女人，有D時候都會諗吓事業。
SAMMY:	我仲以為你哋留喺美國係想過D lay back D嘅生活添。
TANG:	梗係唔係，就係嚟到美國先要搏，美國喎，everything is possible。如果唔係D人做咩爭住嚟？如果唔係點解佢領事館咁寸人都仲嚟排隊做簽證？因為喺呢度搵錢係唔同架。香港D有錢佬最多咪住半山，呢度？有錢可以買起成個Neverland……金融海嘯喎，都唔知浸唔浸到佢哋腳踭，唔信你搵日企喺街角，咪仲係咁多limo……知唔知咩係limo？嗰D好長好長嘅車呢，我未見過一個國家，一日之內有咁多limo經過——雖然我唔係去過好多國家。
SAMMY:	OK。我嫁嚟美國嘅理由又多一個。
TANG:	好架，你仲要跳舞添，國際語言吖嘛，想重操故業起碼冇語言障礙先吖。
SAMMY:	係喇，你做咩架？
TANG:	我？……類似Project co-ordinator咁嘅嘢。
SAMMY:	咁虛嘅，唔明。
TANG:	即係睇吓有咩商機，然後搵人投資咁囉，home office，同祕書鬼混嘅機會都冇，你放心啦。

SAMMY   But it's true. I don't understand how you keep your looks…

TANG   Big deal. They don't do anything for me.

SAMMY   You don't need to tell me. I don't believe men are faithful. But I do wish Ling well.

TANG   It's not a question of being faithful. It's a question of focus. Men don't always think only about women. Sometimes, they think about their careers.

SAMMY   I thought you stayed in the US because you wanted a laid-back lifestyle.

TANG   Are you kidding? It's when you're here that you have to really push. This is America, where anything is possible. Otherwise why would people fight to come? Why do people still line up at US embassies for visas when the staff is so rude? Because making a living here is a whole different thing. In Hong Kong, the best place the rich can live is in the Mid-levels. Here? You can buy Neverland if you have the money. The market crash may not even touch these folks. If you don't believe me, stand on a street corner and you'll see so many limos – you know what a limo is, don't you? Those really long cars? I have never seen a country with so many limos driving past a street corner in a single day – though I haven't been to too many countries.

SAMMY   Great. Another reason to get married over here.

TANG   It's nice here. And you're a dancer. That's an international language. If you move here, at least you won't have any language barrier.

SAMMY:	做咩喎，你唔好當正我係間諜至得架。We are friends, ok?
TANG:	OK。
SAMMY:	咁你今日咁得閒嘅？依家做緊D咩project呀？
TANG:	我……
SAMMY:	做咩呀？商業秘密嚟架？唔講得架？
TANG:	……唔係。我依家做緊個project係關於上網訂購中國製浴室用品嘅，中國D料平吖嘛，趁有門路運過嚟美國賣囉，呢度D人好捨得掟錢裝修。
SAMMY:	哦……聽起上嚟唔錯吖，好似會發達咁。
TANG:	係？
SAMMY:	嗯……
TANG:	idea好有鬼用咩，要有人投資先得架。好似上次咁，我度到條門路搞車仔麵店，遲咗少少之嘛，就俾人開到成行成市。

SAMMY   Speaking of which, what do you do?

TANG   Me? …Sort of like a project coordinator. That kind of thing.

SAMMY   That's pretty vague. I don't get it.

TANG   It means I look for business opportunities and then find investors for them. I keep a home office, so I can't even cheat with my secretary. You can stop worrying.

SAMMY   C'mon, I'm not a spy. We're friends, OK?

TANG   OK.

SAMMY   But you're sorta free today. What kind of project are you working on now?

TANG   I…

SAMMY   What? Is it a secret? You can't tell me?

TANG   …No. I'm working on a project about online purchasing for bathroom fixtures made in China. Materials are cheap in China. I thought I'd sell them in the US if I can find a means of shipping. People here are willing to spend money on renovation.

SAMMY   Oh…Sounds like a good idea, you could get rich.

TANG   Think so?

SAMMY   Mm hmm…

TANG   Well, a good idea is useless without investors. Take the last time, for instance, I came up with an idea for noodles-on-a-cart. But I was a little slow to move and the market became saturated with it.

SAMMY: 車仔麵？你係咪話好似唐人街嗰間香港站呀？我喺Manhattan都有食過──

TANG: 咪係嗰隻囉。諗起就激氣。係我諗到先架！一年前我企喺唐人街突然間靈機一動：呢度咩唐餐都有係冇車仔麵，你諗吓：車仔麵成本低，而且勝在咩呀？配搭有限、做法簡單、價廉物美，如果打早餐、茶餐其實冇乜競爭，搬佢入舖整到靚靚仔仔再標榜杯絲襪奶茶，連fortune cookies都慳返……呢盤生意有得做架。雖然話華人市場，但係美國咁多省份有咁多條唐人街，生意好起上嚟一條街開幾間連鎖式咁開……不過有啦，個大陸佬話考慮吓，過咗幾個月俾人開咗，眼白白睇住人發達。

SAMMY: 咁又真係幾激氣嘅……不過唔緊要啦！嗰個搞唔成搞呢個囉，還掂你已經有idea。唔會次次都俾人捷足先登嘅！今次追緊D啦。

【*稍頓*】

得嘅得嘅。

TANG: 承你貴言。

SAMMY: 咁你呢次搵到人投資未呀？

TANG: ……

SAMMY: 做咩呀？

TANG: ……其實原本我約咗人晏晝傾嘢……不過阿Ling──

SAMMY: 唔係嘛？！佢叫你推咗呀？為咗我呀？

TANG: 我call咗老細改時間囉……不過佢未覆。

SAMMY   Noodles-on-a-cart? You mean like Hong Kong Station in Chinatown? I ate at one of those in Manhattan.

TANG   Yeah, like that. I get so pissed when I think about it. I came up with that idea first. The inspiration hit me a year ago when I was standing in the middle of Chinatown. There're all kinds of Chinese cuisines here, except for noodles-on-a-cart. Think about it. It's low cost, limited menu, so what's the winning strategy? Simple assembly and cheap materials. There's no competition for breakfast and lunch runs. Why not move it into a shop with nice decor? Top it off with a cup of "Stocking Milk Tea", and you can save on the fortune cookies. That's a profitable business. True, it's only targeted towards the Chinese population, but there are so many Chinatowns in so many states. If business is good, you can open up a few branches on the same street. ... But it's all gone. That guy from China said he'd think about it. A few months later, someone else started the business and got rich on it.

SAMMY   Well, that's annoying, true ... But, never mind. That one fell through so work on this one. You already have an idea. It isn't possible that someone will steal your idea every single time. Go for it. (*Slight pause.*) You can do it.

TANG   I hope you're right.

SAMMY   So have you found investors yet? What's wrong?

TANG   Actually, I had an appointment this afternoon, but Ling...

SAMMY   No! She asked you to cancel it? For me?

TANG   I called the boss to reschedule... but he hasn't called me back.

SAMMY: 唔好咁啦唔該！你哋真係老土！崔巧玲真係老土！

TANG: 唔係嘅，我都想陪吓你——

SAMMY: 夠喇香港人，我知人情係紙咁薄喇，但係我講咗好多次：我自己留喺屋企係OK架。

TANG: 但係我驚阿Ling——

SAMMY: 你去啦，我今晚同佢講。

TANG: 你一個人留喺屋企我都唔係咁放心——

SAMMY: Oh come on——

TANG: 一係咁——如果你唔介意……我車埋你去，你喺嗰頭行吓，咁今晚阿Ling返嚟我就話……因為你想出town行吓，所以我就車你落去……其實都冇必要同佢講……我諗佢放工之前我哋都返到……

【*稍頓*】

SAMMY: ……是但啦，總之唔好俾我阻住你……噴，你哋真係老土。

TANG: 唔係嘅，大家嘅出發點都係好嘅。

【*二人相對而笑*】

點呀？掛住講，有得食未架？

【*燈漸暗*】

SAMMY   Please, don't do that on my account. You guys are crazy. Ling is impossible.

TANG   No... I want to keep you company.

SAMMY   That's enough, you "Hong-Kongers". I know your hospitality is sincere, but how many times do I have to tell you, I am OK staying home by myself.

TANG   But I'm afraid Ling...

SAMMY   Go! I'll speak with her tonight.

TANG   I'm worried about you here alone.

SAMMY   Oh, come on...

TANG   How about this... If you don't mind, I'll take you with me. You can walk around there. And tonight I'll tell Ling that... You wanted to go to town, so I brought you... Actually, we don't have to tell her at all...we'll be home before she gets back from work... (*Slight pause.*)

SAMMY   Whatever... Just don't let me stop you... You guys are impossible.

TANG   No, we mean well. (*They turn to each other and laugh.*) Hey, what happened to the breakfast?

(*Lights fade out.*)

第三場

【*黃昏，屋內多了幾只亂放的空杯，花園傳來音樂聲、笑聲*】

TANG: ……喂，試吓喉下面燒上嚟先……我去攞埋D炭精，我記得屋企好似仲剩返D——

【*玲招呼明從大門進，正感到奇怪，Tang從花園出來*】

玲: 搞咩呀？

TANG: 燒嘢食囉……呢位係？

玲: 我舊同事明哥；阿Tang，我老公。你哋想BBQ又唔話我知嘅？等我仲買晒餸……

TANG: 我有留口訊俾你架。

玲: ……個手提漏咗喺公司——邊個嚟咗？

【*Zoë從花園出*】

ZOË: 鄧太太！好久沒見呀！【*向花園高呼*】老公！鄧太太回來啦……【*熱情地走向玲*】嘩，看你肚子都這麼大了！男孩女孩？什麼時候生呢？這小鄧真是的，你有了喜都不告訴我們一聲，早知道我就從國內給你帶點什麼補品回來，哎呀鄧太太你不要客氣，我們俗話說得好：出門靠朋友，我跟小鄧雖然是朋友，可我是把他看成親弟弟一樣——咦？這位是？

【*玲向Tang擺出一副「為什麼她在這裡？！」的姿態*】

明哥: 你好，我是沈建明——叫我阿明好了。

<u>SCENE 3</u>

(*Dusk. There are a few more empty glasses around the house. Music and laughter are heard from the garden.*)

TANG   Hey, try starting the flame from below. I'll get some charcoal. We should have some left over.

(*Ling welcomes Ming to her house as they enter the front door. She feels strange. Tang enters from the garden.*)

LING   What's going on?

TANG   We're having a barbecue. This is…?

LING   My former colleague, Ming. Tang, my husband. Why didn't you tell me you were gonna barbecue? I bought all this food…

TANG   I left you a message.

LING   I left my cell phone at the office. Who's here? (*Zoë enters from the garden.*)

ZOË   Mrs. Tang. It's been a while. (*Towards the garden.*) Honey, Mrs. Tang is home… (*Passionately towards Ling.*) Wow, look how big your tummy is. Is it a boy or a girl? When are you due? Tang, you didn't tell us you had good news. If I'd known, I would've brought over some herbal tonic from China. No reason to be shy. We have a great saying "Depend on friends when abroad". Mr. Tang and I are such good friends. He's like my younger brother. Oh? This is…? (*Ling signals Tang to say "what is she doing here?"*)

MING   Hello. I'm Shen Jian Ming. Call me Ming.

ZOÉ:	Zoë，我叫Zoë，聽你口音應該是⋯⋯【*閩南語*】台灣人？
明哥：	【*閩南語*】對，我是台灣人。
ZOÉ:	我就知道！我有好多台灣朋友，一聽就知道⋯⋯
明哥：	【*向玲*】亞玲，你們今日有朋友，我會不會打擾了——
玲：	你——
ZOÉ:	不打擾！既然是鄧家的朋友，大家就是自己人！留下來吃飯，今晚兒我請客——我們在唐人街買了好多海鮮回來燒烤，多得吃不完的！而且保證好吃！我叫我老公選了最大那只龍蝦，到現在還鮮蹦活跳的，你要不要看看？來來來，過來看！來呀！過來看看大龍蝦⋯⋯
玲：	得喇Zoë，我諗明哥有見過龍蝦，佢今日喺L.A.揸車過嚟，你俾佢坐低飲杯茶先。
ZOÉ:	你從洛杉磯過來的？哎喲我好喜歡洛杉磯這個城市，每次過去我都叫我老公帶我去那個環球影城！每一次都去！我特愛看那個科幻製作特輯，太好看了！阿明你有看過嗎？

【*Patrick從從花園出*】

PATRICK:	完了。
ZOÉ:	老公！這是鄧太太的朋友阿明，從台灣來的。
PATRICK:	台灣？今天怎麼搞的？兩岸三地的人都來了，小鄧你厲害，中國在你鄧家小小的屋頂下不費一兵一力就統一了⋯⋯喂——有買股票嗎？

ZOË	Zoë. I'm Zoë. From your accent, I gather you are… (*In Taiwanese dialect*) Taiwanese?
MING	Yes, Taiwanese.
ZOË	I knew it. We have many Taiwanese friends. I knew it, the moment you opened your mouth.
MING	(*To Ling.*) You have guests today. I don't want to intrude…
LING	You…
ZOË	Not at all! A friend of the Tangs is a friend of ours. Stay for dinner. Our treat tonight. We bought a lot of seafood from Chinatown to barbecue. Like, a ton of food. We guarantee it'll be good. I told my husband to pick the biggest lobster. It's so fresh, it's still jumping. Wanna see? Come, come, come… come see. Come! Take a look at the giant lobster.
LING	Oh, Zoë, I'm sure Ming has seen lobsters before. He drove up from LA today. Let him sit and have a cup of tea first.
ZOË	You're from LA? Oh, I love LA. Every time I go there I ask my husband to take me to Universal Studios. And we go every time. I especially love the special effects show. It's amazing. Have you seen it, Ming? (*Patrick enters from the garden.*)
PATRICK	It's over.
ZOË	Honey, this is Mrs. Tang's friend, Ming, from Taiwan.
PATRICK	Taiwan? What's happening here? We have representatives from both shores and three lands! Tang, you're really something. You have managed to unite China under your roof without lifting a finger… So, do you play the stock market?

明哥：　　　沒有沒有，還好不會。

PATRICK：　我們也剛好放了，逃過一刧，你説，大陸出毒牛奶，美國出毒股票，這世界還有安全的國家嗎？

ZOË：　　　老公老公，你剛走出來的時候説什麼完了？

PATRICK：　我説那火呀，滅了！這危急關頭你們只顧談天説地，該拿炭精的沒拿，該拿報紙的又不拿，那火種可不就滅了嗎？

TANG：　　我依家去攞。

PATRICK：　我説別「攞」了，都滅了，倒不如給我弄點什麼喝喝？我要那個白白的叫巴什麼——

TANG：　　得，Barbara吖嘛。

PATRICK：　唉，剛才那煙把我嗆得都難受了……

ZOË：　　　哎呀老公，人家不是故意的，見了新朋友嘛就多聊兩句……

PATRICK：　我就知道你，成事不足敗事有餘。

ZOË：　　　哎喲，怎麼在新朋友面前這樣説我呢你？

PATRICK：　我説錯了嗎？要不是你提議自己動手燒烤我們現在已經在餐廳舒舒服服的吃了，哪用費那麼多功夫？説起來還真有點餓，阿玲，先隨便弄點什麼出來吃吃吧……

ZOË：　　　人家打算順便看看小鄧的房子嘛，大家認識了這麼久還沒登門拜訪的，太沒誠意了吧……唉，早知道是那麼費神，就僱個人回來給我們燒。現在龍蝦還沒宰呢！

MING	No, fortunately.
PATRICK	We just sold as well. Missed the crash. Honestly, between the Chinese poison milk powder scandal and the American stock market crash, is any country safe anymore?
ZOË	Honey, you said something's over? What were you — ?
PATRICK	The fire. It's gone out. This is a critical moment and you're all sitting chatting. Nobody went for charcoal. Nobody brought any newspaper. So – the fire's out.
TANG	I'll get some.
PATRICK	Forget it. It's out. Why don't you get me a drink? I want that ba… ba… what-do-you-call-it.
TANG	Sure. Barbara.
PATRICK	The smoke really hurt my throat.
ZOË	Honey, I'm really sorry. We met this new friend and started chatting.
PATRICK	It's all your fault.
ZOË	Oh! How can you say that about me in front of our new friend?
PATRICK	It's true, isn't it? If you didn't suggest barbecuing, we'd be sitting comfortably in a restaurant eating by now. We wouldn't have wasted all this effort. Speaking of which, I'm getting hungry. Ling, make us a snack first, will you?
ZOË	I wanted to have a look at Tang's house. We've never visited his home in all the time we've known him. Very unfriendly of us. We should've hired someone to barbecue if I'd known it was so much work. The lobster's still alive.

SAMMY: 【花園傳來】有沒有報紙呀？

PATRICK: 別吵了！學一下人家阿玲的朋友，火滅心不死，標準香港人的拼搏精神。

玲： 【*站在花園門口叫*】由佢啦張詠兒，我劏埋隻龍蝦先幫你搞。

PATRICK: 讓她玩吧我看她搞得廷愉快的……對了阿玲，這件好東西從哪兒冒出來的？香港回歸以後不是很流行學普通話的嗎？想不到香港人現在說普通話還是那麼難聽！

ZOË: 是呀鄧太太，你這朋友真是搞笑，我都叫她說廣東話了，我們經常看港劇，聽得懂，可她硬要說普通話，說得亂七八糟的……給我笑了整整一個下午……

玲： 你帶埋張詠兒去開會咩？

TANG: 係呀，我後來都係決定去開會，費時Sammy自己一個留喺屋企，咪車埋佢落唐人街行吓——

PATRICK: 撒謊！撒謊！你老公是小壞蛋！故意找個「靚女」假裝路過，說什麼打完招呼就走，怎知道一坐下來就不得了，對我軟硬兼用！不斷說小鄧的project這裡好那裡好，噢，我想起來了，真有點像人家鳳凰衛視說的那些商業欺騙案。

ZOË: 你別聽他亂講，是我叫森米留下的，兩個大男人談生意，我叫森米留下來陪我聊天……我們還去聯合廣場shopping哩！

PATRICK	Never mind. You should learn from Ling's friend. The fire is out but her heart's still burning strong. Typical of Hong Kong people. They're very tenacious.
LING	(*Stands and shouts at garden door.*) Leave it, Cheung Wing Yee. Let me kill the lobster and I'll come help you.
PATRICK	Oh, let her have her fun with it. So Ling, where did your little friend come from? I thought since the Handover, Hong Kong people would've grown fluent in Putonghua. I can't believe their Putonghua is still so awful.
ZOË	That's right, Mrs. Tang. Your friend is hilarious. I told her to speak Cantonese. We watch Hong Kong soap operas. We can understand Cantonese. But she insists on speaking Putonghua, which she simply cannot… She made me laugh so hard all afternoon, I was in stitches…
LING	You took Cheung Wing Yee to your meeting?
TANG	Yeah, I decided to go to my meeting. I didn't want Sammy to be home by herself so I took her with me so she could walk around Chinatown.
PATRICK	Liar. Liar. Your husband is a smooth operator. He brings this hot date with him and pretends to be "passing by". Says something about just wanting to say hi. But as soon as they sat down, I was done for. She kept going on and on about how good Tang's project was. Just like those infomercials on Phoenix TV.
ZOË	Don't listen to him. I told Sammy to stay. While the men talked business. I asked Sammy to keep me company. We even went shopping in Union Square.

TANG:	係呀，Sammy同Zoë好啱傾，Sammy都好似玩得好開心咁！
PATRICK:	就是，森米跟我老婆話可多呢，兩個人在前面嘰嘰喳喳嘻嘻哈哈的，喂，你們到底在笑什麼呢？
ZOË:	沒什麼，就香港那些花邊新聞。森米不是跳舞嗎，原來她也去演唱會伴舞，所以啊，她知道好多明星的祕密！
PATRICK:	是嗎？什麼祕密？
ZOË:	不能說的！
PATRICK:	嘖，那有什麼關係？
ZOË:	傳出怎麼辦，害人家森米丟了工作——
PATRICK:	嘖！老公叫都不說？說！

【*Zoë在Patrick耳邊細語*】

……什麼？黎明買了一頭狗送樂基兒？誰是樂基兒？

ZOË:	去，跟你說也是白說！鄧太太，森米說她下禮拜就回去，怎麼這樣匆忙？叫她多住幾天，也去我們帕羅奧圖（Palo Alto）那邊逛逛，你說好不好？
玲：	你自己問佢。
ZOË:	森米這人真好玩，又隨和……對了鄧太太，聽說她還沒有對象呢，你說怎麼可能呢？人長得這麼漂亮！
玲：	我唔知，你自己問佢。

TANG Oh yeah. Sammy and Zoë really got along well. Those two were chit chatting and laughing… What were you laughing at?

ZOË Nothing, we were just gossiping about the Hong Kong tabloids. Sammy is a dancer. She works in pop concerts so she knows a lot of dish about the stars.

PATRICK Really? What dish?

ZOË I can't say.

PATRICK Why not?

ZOË If it got out, it could hurt Sammy's career.

PATRICK I'm your husband. Tell me! (*Zoë whispers in Patrick's ear.*) What? Leon Lai bought a dog for Gaile? (*Tang places a drink in front of Patrick.*) Who's Gaile?

ZOË Jeez, what's the point of telling you? Mrs. Tang, Sammy said she's going back next week. What's the hurry? Tell her to stay a few more days. She can come over to our place in Palo Alto. I can take her to see the Palo Alto redwood trees. They are over 1,000 years old and incredibly beautiful. Don't you think that's a good idea?

LING Ask her yourself.

ZOË Sammy is so much fun. And easy going. Oh, right, Mrs. Tang, I hear she's still single. How can that be? Such a pretty girl.

LING I don't know. Ask her yourself.

PATRICK: 你以為每一個女人都像你這麼好命，沒本事卻遇上好老公？我這個老婆啊，命好得不得了，在家裡有老爸養、嫁出去有老公疼，糊里糊塗的還讓她出國哩——

ZOË: 老公呀，就是自己嫁得好才知道嫁得好的重要！不如我們給她介紹林嘉——林嘉是我們省書記的兒子，來美國開公司，四十不到就擁有一間過百人的工廠，算年青有為了！

PATRICK: 什麼年青有為，不就靠他老爸……

ZOË: 我這個老公，總是找機會強調自己是白手興家。

PATRICK: 可不是？我們這一代是社會歷練出來的，哪像這群ABCD，飯來張口錢來攤手——我今天跟你説那個美膳坊的太子爺就這個臭樣，不就過來幾年嘛，滿口英語，不分尊卑，老俞那酒家早晚讓他給敗了……

ZOË: 人家在討論森米的對象，你發什麼牢騷……要不劉飛！年紀是大了一點，而且離過婚，但是結過婚的男人好，有經驗，他那家印刷廠有好多大客戶……

明哥: 阿玲，我突然想起公司有事情，我看我還是先回去——

PATRICK   You think every woman is as lucky as you, good for nothing yet able to find a fine husband? My wife is so lucky. At home, she has a father who's loaded. In marriage, she has a doting husband who lets her move out of the country. (*Pulling Zoe away from Ling*) Not so close, you'll get your clothes dirty!

ZOË   Honey, I married well so I know the importance of finding a good husband. I'm trying to be helpful. Let's introduce Lin Ka to her. Lin Ka is the son of our provincial secretary. He started his own business in the States. Not yet 40, but he owns a factory with over 100 employees. That's impressive for a young man.

PATRICK   Impressive? It's all his old man's doing.

ZOË   Still, he has to have perseverance. My husband never passes up an opportunity to let everyone know that he started with nothing.

PATRICK   But it's true. Our generation had to learn everything hands-on, not like the "ABCs" of today. They're spoon-fed. That restaurant, "Fine Meals", I was talking about? The owner's son is exactly like that. He came over a few years ago. Now he'll only speak English. Has no respect for his elders. Sooner or later, he'll lose that restaurant.

ZOË   We're talking about a man for Sammy. What are you blabbering about? How about Liu Fei? He is a little older and divorced. But a divorced man is good. He's experienced. His printing company has lots of big clients. Have you heard of Hallmark and Disney, Ming? They're his clients. All American name brands…

MING   Really? …Ling, I just remembered I had some business to attend to. Maybe I should go…

ZOË: 不行！什麼事情都明天做，反正都來了！今天兒我請客誰都不能走，要不就是不賞面！

PATRICK: 說的是，你無論如何也要留下——「沒有台灣，中國便不完整了」——哈……

ZOË: 拜託！不要再講這種笑話！

PATRICK: 怕什麼？這裡是美國，只談經濟利益，談政治也是笑話，誰會介意一個笑話？

TANG: 明哥你唔好介意，Patrick好鍾意講笑，不過台灣人出名身份意識強，我哋都唔好攞呢D嘢講笑喇Patrick。

PATRICK: 唉呀，我是看大家都移了民，隔岸觀火才開開玩笑……不過話說回來，在這身份問題上台灣人還真頑固，不像香港人，最滑頭。

TANG: 我哋適應能力高啫。歷史造成嘅，唔通下下改朝換代都撐到恆？如果所謂嘅身份意識係阻礙緊我融入新生活，我就寧願改變自己去適應環境。

明哥: 我覺得那是因為你們香港人重視經濟效益超過一切。

TANG: 嗯？

明哥: 或者說是一種結果——因為不想探究身份問題，所以才向經濟發展。

ZOË No! Whatever it is, leave it for tomorrow. You're here already. My treat today so nobody leaves. If you leave, you're not giving me face.

PATRICK That's right. You must stay. "Without Taiwan, China is not complete" !

ZOË Oh, please, don't joke about that.

PATRICK What? This is America. We only talk about money. Politics is a joke. Nobody minds a joke.

TANG Ming, don't let Patrick get to you. He's a big joker. But Taiwanese are very sensitive about their identity. We shouldn't joke about that.

PATRICK Oh, c'mon. We're all immigrants. We can laugh being so far away. But when it comes to identity, the Taiwanese are very stubborn. Unlike Hong Kong people, who are very slick.

TANG We're just very adaptable. History made us that way. What were we going to do, fight every change of government that came along? If a sense of identity means I can't adjust to a new environment, I'd rather change myself and adapt.

MING That's because you think economic advantages are more important than everything else.

TANG: 我會咁睇囉，有時唔需要將身份問題睇得太重，Patrick話齋大家移咗民隔岸觀火咁我至敢講，你都見到大勢所趨啦，好話唔好聽呢D身份問題嘅爭拗喺歷史洪流算得係咩？喺大文化裡面又算得係咩？如果註定會消失或者被歸一，掌握一D可以控制嘅嘢譬如話經濟命脈咁，唔係更加務實咩？

明哥: ……也許你說得對……這些身份問題的爭論什至爭取，在歷史洪流裡面不算什麼，一百年、五百年之後再看它，也不過是一個小小浪花而已。但我覺得就是在這小浪花裡如何掙扎便體現出人性的尊嚴，我想我們是站在完全不同的觀點去看這件事情，你說的是生存，而我說的是如何生存得有尊嚴。

　　　【靜場】

ZOË: 哎呀！我這搭不上嘴才叫沒有尊嚴！【大家都乾笑了】都不要談這種嚴肅的話題了！對了阿明，您是做哪一行的——我猜！你一定是當老師的！

明哥: ……我是做船務的……是家小公司。

ZOË: 別這樣說，潛力最重要。我們以前還不是小公司做出來……那您成家了沒有……看您踏實踏實的，該成家了吧？

明哥: 【不自覺看看玲】……還沒有……

ZOË: 吖？真想不到呢……

PATRICK: ……你剛才說你做船務？

明哥: 是的。

TANG   It's my opinion. I don't think the question of identity needs to be such a big deal. Just like Patrick said, we're all immigrants. You see how fast things are changing. What's the point of arguing about identity in the grand scheme of things? Is it relevant to the big picture? Given the choice between fitting in or going extinct, isn't holding onto something you can control, like economics, much more practical?

MING   …Maybe you're right…. Arguing about identity or struggling against the historical tide hardly matters. In 100 years, or 500 years, it will seem like a tiny splash in the ocean of larger events. But that splash is the struggle for human dignity. We are looking at the problem from completely different points of view. You're talking about surviving. I'm talking about surviving with dignity. (*Quiet.*)

ZOË   You know, I'm the one who feels undignified because this conversation is way over my head. (*Everyone laughs.*) Let's not talk about such serious subjects. Ming, what do you do? Let me guess. You must be a teacher.

MING   …I'm in shipping… It's a small company.

ZOË   Don't be so humble. Potential is the key. We used to have a small company too… Then are you married? …You're very down-to-earth. You must be married.

MING   (*Unconsciously looks at Ling.*) Not yet…

ZOË   What? I can't believe that…

PATRICK   You say you're in shipping?

MING   Yes.

ZOË:　　　　天呀我真大意……哎呀！

PATRICK:　　小鄧，他做船務的呢……

ZOË:　　　　……鄧太太你請他來是跟Sammy相親……

玲：　　　　得架喇Zoë，我咁啱請佢上嚟食飯架咋，冇咩架……

ZOË:　　　　那你還坐在這裡幹啥？快出去！你快出去見見她！哎我弄得你不好意思啦對吧？還老遠從L.A.開車來呢——

PATRICK:　　你安靜一下！我在問他話呢！

　　　　　　【頓時靜下】

　　　　　　來，阿明，我來請教你一件事情。

明哥：　　　不用客氣，不用客氣——

PATRICK:　　不！這事情可要緊呢……小鄧幫我看上一門生意——

TANG:　　　Patrick，依家傾呢D嘢會唔會早咗D——

ZOË	Oh my god, I'm such a fool. You're here today because... Oh no!
PATRICK	Tang, he's in shipping...
ZOË	Mrs. Tang, you asked him here to ... I am so clueless ... Don't just sit around! Go outside! Go meet her outside.
LING	It's fine, Zoë, don't worry about him. It's nothing. I just invited him home for dinner...
ZOË	Oh, I've made this awkward, haven't I? And you drove all the way from LA...
PATRICK	Will you keep it down? I want to talk to him! (*Instant silence.*) Ming, come, I need to ask you about something.
MING	Please, I'm not qualified.
PATRICK	No, this is very important. Tang has found a business opportunity for me...
TANG	Patrick, isn't it a bit premature to talk about this now?...

PATRICK: 做生意要多聽聽各方面的意見，是這樣的，我以前在國內是做生意的，現在我就退休來三藩市，兒子上西雅圖唸書。在這裡人生路不熟，語言又不通，本來不打算再搞什麼，但是在唐人街飲茶遇上這小鄧，他十年來幫老外打工，算是對這個國家比較熟悉，我就跟他說，你看看，看有啥門路，我當做投資，反正這年代錢放銀行更危險……去年他說開麵館子，我想，嘩，飲食業，多辛苦呀，我幾十歲的人，在國內總算做過高檔生意，反而到美國來開麵館，還不笑話人？所以我【*不住的搖頭*】——吖，這次他提議搞浴室用品，過得去，還說要弄什麼上網……上網……

TANG: 網上購物。

PATRICK: 網上購物，對，網上購物。把國內的浴室用品運過來賣，現在不是流行什麼上網嗎？我們在國內低價生產，運過來高價出售……我說小鄧，不錯，這下子有瞄頭了。不過上網這東西我不熟悉，我意思是說，人家在電腦上卡啦卡啦的就能付錢？安全嗎？會不會運了過來才發現收不到錢？

明哥: 這個你不用擔心，現在網路購物十分流行，好多交易都是在網路完成的。

PATRICK   In business, we have to ask everyone's advice. I think Ming here knows his business. No harm asking him. It's like this. I used to have my own business in China. When my son went to school in Seattle, I retired and came to San Francisco. I didn't know anyone and I didn't speak the language so I didn't plan to do much over here. But then I met Tang over dim sum in Chinatown. He's worked for Westerners for ten years, so he knows this country. So I said to him, you look for something and I'll invest in it. After all, keeping your money in a bank these days isn't any safer… Last year, he suggested opening a noodle shop and I thought, restaurant business, that's hard work. I'm not young anymore. In China, you could say that I was in a high profile kind of business. How can I open a noodle shop in America?! People would laugh at me. So I… (*Shakes his head.*) … Well, now he's suggesting bathroom fixtures. Sounds promising. And he said something about online…

TANG   Online shopping?

PATRICK   Online shopping, yes, right. Sell bathroom fixtures made in China. This online shopping is very popular now, right? We can produce cheaply in China and sell high over here. So I think Tang's got the right idea this time. But I know nothing about the Internet. What I'm getting at is, people can click a few buttons and buy stuff on the computer? Is that safe? What if we ship the merchandise here but we can't collect the money?

MING   You don't have to worry about that. Online shopping is very common now. Lots of consumer products are sold that way.

TANG:	咪係，依家係網絡世界嘅年代，咩都可以喺屋企搞掂。
PATRICK:	那……該怎麼弄呢？
TANG:	唔使我哋煩架，登記間公司，銀行自然會幫我哋做，Patrick，都係嗰句，你唔使諗咁多嘢，呢D技術性問題我哋可以從長計議。
PATRICK:	你老説這句，就要我儘快拿錢。
明哥：	事實上外面真有公司在做這方面的配套，你可以讓他們辦。反而你們要擔心的是運輸方面的問題……
TANG:	其實都冇咩好擔心嘅——
PATRICK:	什麼問題？
明哥：	因為美國比較麻煩，每個州都有不同的法律和進口稅，如果進出商品，除非你們只做加州，不然要小心，我們好多客戶都……
TANG:	我問過熟人，運費嘅差額應該唔大。
明哥：	對，運費差額是沒有很大，但是如果加上進口稅，差別就可以很大，而你們如果零售價格偏低的話，非常有可能接下訂單以後才發現不夠錢繳稅，到時候退錢又不是……出貨又不是……不過也不是那麼——

TANG	I told you. It's the Internet age. You can do everything at home.
PATRICK	How does it work?
TANG	We don't have to do anything. You register a company and a bank will take care of the rest. Patrick, don't worry about this now. We'll go over the tech stuff later.
PATRICK	You keep saying that because you want my money.
MING	It's true that there are companies out there that specialize in this service. You can let them take care of it. What you do need to worry about, though, is the shipping …
TANG	There's really nothing to worry about…
PATRICK	What's the problem?
MING	The US is a bit tricky. Every state has different laws and import taxes. With import and export, unless you only do business in California, you have to be careful. We have many clients… well..
TANG	I asked around. The difference in shipping costs isn't that big.
MING	True. The difference is small. But the difference in the import tax is huge. If your wholesale prices are very low, you may find you can't pay the import tax after receiving your orders. By then, you wouldn't know if you should refund the money or send out the merchandise. But maybe… It's not that…

PATRICK: 喂喂喂，你怎能這樣大意？人家隨便聽聽就發現的重大問題你好像想都沒想到似的？還告訴我什麼資料齊全？

明哥: ……現在談這個可能太早吧，大概——

PATRICK: 不早了，都來要錢了！

ZOË: 老公，別嚷嚷，都還沒拿錢呢！。

PATRICK: 幸好沒拿！要拿出來不已經虧了！

ZOË: 哎，你這人真是——

TANG: Patrick講得啱嘅，我再check吓，check清楚下個禮拜再同你哋報價。十拿九穩先叫你哋做，風險大D我都唔會叫你哋落注，唔通攞你哋D退休金嚟較飛咩……

PATRICK: 這種態度就對了……你再下一點功夫，我從廣州回來咱們再談。

TANG: 你又返廣州咩？

PATRICK: 沒辦法，老朋友娶媳婦兒，硬要請我回去，這次好大的排場，延開二百桌，聽說女家跟人大有什麼聯繫，也好，湊湊熱鬧去，順便辦些年貨，你也知道，這唐人街沒什麼好東西……喂小鄧，別著急，我跟你說，你做生意的經驗淺，每一步都要心思細密，尤其現在這種經濟環境，是機會也是危機，可不能鬧著玩……

PATRICK   Hey, how'd you miss that one? We casually tell him our plan and he points out a huge problem, just like that. Did you even consider this? And you keep telling me you have all the information.

MING   …It's premature to discuss this now…

PATRICK   No, it's not. Not when he's asking me to put out money.

ZOË   Honey, don't raise your voice. He hasn't taken any money yet.

PATRICK   Lucky for us he hasn't. If he had, we would have lost it all by now.

ZOË   Oh, you're so…

TANG   Patrick is right. I should do more research. Let me get back to you next week with a new quote. I won't let you invest unless I'm absolutely certain. I wouldn't let you take risks. You think I'd squander your life savings?

PATRICK   That's the right attitude. Do a little more work on it. We can talk again when I come back from Guangzhou.

TANG   You're going back to China?

PATRICK   No choice. My old friend's son is getting married. He insists I go back for it. This is a huge affair. Two hundred tables. I heard the bride is somehow related to someone in the National People's Congress. Should be fun. And we can do some New Year shopping. You know, there's not much to buy in Chinatown. Tang, be patient. Listen to me, you don't have much business experience. You must think before every step, especially in the current economic climate. Opportunity is also where danger lurks. It's not a game.

ZOË: 好了好了！這簡單的道理人家鄧太太還不會提醒他？

PATRICK: 對了，我說阿玲呀……我在想嘛，本金我們各出一半好不好？反正你老公說得一定賺似的，不如你也投資一份——

TANG: Patrick你唔使問佢，佢唔識架——

PATRICK: 什麼不懂？我們都談了這麼久還不懂——阿玲，老公搞生意老婆應該支持，咱們商量商量，怎樣安排才是公平公正——

【*Sammy興奮進場*】

SAMMY: 【*疑似國語*】各位，沒花沒假童叟無欺，整個過程沒火機、沒炭精的，只靠兩條柴跟一堆草——I made a fire!

玲: 個爐有打火機。

PATRICK: 哎呀……在我這裡。

SAMMY: 我都知道是你玩嘢！

【*Patrick和Zoë都顯得很愉快*】

Anyway，個火已經準備好，let's BBQ！

ZOË: 看我們森米多厲害呀！

SAMMY: 當然！

ZOË: 森米，你還沒認識明哥呢，他老遠從洛杉磯開車來吃這頓飯……

SAMMY: Hello明哥！

明哥: 你好。

ZOË   All right, all right. Surely, Mrs. Tang will remind her husband of such simple principles.

PATRICK   Oh right, Ling, I was thinking. Why don't we go in 50-50? Your husband tells me it's a sure profit. Why don't you invest…

TANG   Patrick, don't bother. She doesn't understand…

ZOË   (*To Patrick*) Let the two of them discuss it themselves.

PATRICK   Doesn't understand? We've been talking about it for half a day. Ming, you can think about it too. Look, Ling, your husband wants to go into business. You should support him. We can work out a fair deal. (*Sammy enters with excitement.*)

SAMMY   (*In poor Putonghua*) Everybody. I'm not kidding. All it took was two tree branches and a pile of grass. No lighter and charcoal – I made a fire!

LING   There's a lighter next to the barbecue.

PATRICK   Oh… I've got it!

SAMMY   I knew you had it. (*Patrick and Zoë seem very happy.*) Lucky my stubbornness is good for something. Anyway, the fire is ready. Let's barbecue!

Zoë   Sammy, you're amazing.

SAMMY   Yes, I am.

ZOË   Sammy, have you met Ming? He came from LA for this meal. You must serve him well.

SAMMY   Hello, Ming.

MING   Hello.

SAMMY: 唔係嘛，又係國語人？！

【大家邊介紹談笑邊離去，剩下Tang和玲】

TANG: 唔該你，唔好成晚嬲埋口面。

玲: 你唔好喺度嘥時間，佢根本喺度玩你——

TANG: 殊！你好喇你，唔關你事呀！

玲: 唔關我事？你帶得佢哋上嚟就關我事，你應承過唔帶佢哋上嚟！

TANG: 你估我想架？咁佢問到，你個朋友又一口應承⋯⋯何況你都開始叫人上嚟——

玲: 點同呢——

TANG: 我依家冇心情同你拗——

SAMMY: Hey！

【Sammy進，見氣氛奇怪】

做咩呀？

玲: 冇。

TANG: 我出去先。唔該晒你呀Sammy。

SAMMY: ⋯⋯唔使客氣。

【Sammy看著Tang離去】

玲: 入嚟想要咩？

SAMMY: 佢哋問有冇辣椒油同碟，Zoë話唔鍾意用紙碟喎，依家D大陸人真係奄尖⋯⋯hey，你今日幾好嘛？返工有冇鐘眼瞓呀？

SAMMY	Oh no, another Putonghua person? (*Everyone talks, laughs and exits as introduction is made, leaving Tang and Ling.*)
TANG	Please, lose the attitude. (*Just about to exit.*)
LING	Don't waste your time. They're just playing with you…
TANG	Shhh! Stop it. It's none of your business.
LING	None of my business? You brought them to my home so that makes it my business. You promised you wouldn't bring them here.
TANG	You think I wanted to? They asked and your friend said "Sure!" Besides, you're the one who invited…
LING	That's different.
TANG	I'm not in the mood to fight …
SAMMY	Hey… (*Sammy enters and sees the awkwardness.*) What's wrong?
LING	Nothing.
TANG	I'm going outside. Thanks, Sammy.
SAMMY	You're welcome. (*Sammy watches Tang exit.*)
LING	What do you want?
SAMMY	They asked for chili sauce and a plate. Zoë doesn't like using paper plates. Mainlanders are so picky now… So, how was your day? Were you tired at work?

玲:　　　……辣椒油……碟。

SAMMY:　　……崔巧玲？你冇乜野吖嘛？

玲:　　　冇呀。

　　　　【Zoë進】

SAMMY:　　咦，Zoë你為什麼不留在外面燒呀？我幫你拿碟
　　　　子了……

ZOË:　　　我喜歡暖和的盤子，鄧太太，你可不可以幫我
　　　　順手暖一下這盤子呢？

　　　　【玲將碟子放進焗爐，調溫開機】

SAMMY:　　我剛剛才說你們大陸人現在真是淹尖呀……

ZOË:　　　哎呀，人家用慣西餐廳的盤子，都是暖和暖和
　　　　的，這一點咱們唐人餐廳就及不上，西方人做
　　　　生意每個細節都照顧週到……

　　　　【靜場】

ZOË:　　　鄧太太你不要介意，我老公說話就是那麼直
　　　　接，我也討厭他那種粗魯的語氣，但是呢……
　　　　他從小打拚，一談到錢連自己的兒子也沒情
　　　　面，要你沒那種想法甭理他，就當他說說傻
　　　　話……可要是你也有興趣的話，大家一起做
　　　　也蠻開心的呀……你想一想，人面都靠我們
　　　　聯繫，阿Tang又說明以後不想出國公幹，
　　　　那就是說國內的事情我們都得自己跑，靠小
　　　　鄧的只是語言和科技……當然，我們也需要
　　　　他，畢竟我們在這邊沒幾個朋友，可這就更
　　　　加要……要……哎呀，我急啥呀？咱們以後
　　　　再從長計議，讓你們夫婦倆先商量商量……真
　　　　是……嗯——那我先拿辣油出去嘍……

　　　　【Zoë離去，Sammy聽得一頭霧水】

LING	Chili sauce… Plate.
SAMMY	Chui Hau Ling, is something wrong?
LING	No. (*Zoë enters.*)
SAMMY	Zoë, why aren't you barbecuing outside? I have your plate here.
ZOË	I like my plates warm. Mrs. Tang, do you mind warming my plate?
SAMMY	I was just saying, you Mainlanders are so picky now.
ZOË	Well, I'm used to the warm, heated plates in Western restaurants. That's where our Chinese restaurants can't compare. Westerners know how to take care of small details in businesses. (*Silence.*) Mrs. Tang, I hope you don't mind. My husband is very plain-spoken. I hate it when he's blunt and rude but… He had to struggle a lot when he was young. He's so insensitive when he talks about money, even to his own son. Don't listen to him. He's full of nonsense… But if you're interested, we could have a good time working together… Think about it. You'll have to rely on our contacts. Tang said he never wants to work abroad again. We'll have to do all the running around in China. Tang will be responsible for overcoming the language barrier and handling the technology… Of course we need him too. After all, we have no friends here so we have to be more… more… Oh, dear, what's the hurry? We can talk about all this later. You and your husband should discuss things first… Honestly… Um… I'll bring the chili sauce outside… (*Zoë exits. Sammy is completely confused.*)

SAMMY:　　佢講咩呀？

玲:　　　　發噏風。

SAMMY:　　今日聽國語真係聽到我頭都wing……唔係喇，
　　　　　一陣我哋隔一陣就閃埋一二便，齋廢噏都好，
　　　　　我要俾大腦門一門機──不過你老公好本事！
　　　　　你今日冇見佢present個樣，幾醒目呀──

玲:　　　　你識咗明哥未呀？

SAMMY:　　個台灣佬？briefly咁識咗啦，好怕醜咁嘅。

玲:　　　　識落就多嘢講架啦。

　　　　　【看到Sammy的領口，幫她扣上】

　　　　　你咁樣人哋點同你講嘢呀？

SAMMY:　　佢對眼同個口唔可以同時運作架咩？

玲:　　　　得，不過你同時開幾個program部腦都郁得慢D
　　　　　啦。

　　　　　【見玲打開焗爐，想接過碟子】

玲:　　　　等等。

　　　　　【玲幫Sammy戴上隔熱手套】

　　　　　同Zoë講叫佢睇熱。

SAMMY:　　知道。【Sammy拿著碟子離開，玲繼續廚房的
　　　　　事務，靜場，好一會只聽見花園的歡笑聲，緊
　　　　　接聲一撕裂人心的尖叫，玲沒有回頭】

　　　　　【燈滅】

SAMMY   What is she talking about?

LING   Bullshit.

SAMMY   I'm dizzy from listening to all this Putonghua today. Later on, I say we get away from them. We can just shoot the shit but I have to let my brain rest. Your husband is so smart. You should have seen him at the presentation. He was great...

LING   Have you met Ming?

SAMMY   The Taiwanese guy? Briefly. Very shy.

LING   He'll talk once you get to know him. (*Sees Sammy's collar and buttons it.*) How is he supposed to talk with you like that?

SAMMY   Can't his eyes and mouth work at the same time?

LING   Sure. But when you've got several programs going, the computer runs a little slower. (*Sammy sees Ling open the oven and proceed to retrieve a plate.*) Wait. (*Ling hands Sammy some oven mittens.*) Tell Zoë to be careful of the hot plate.

SAMMY   I will. (*Sammy exits with the plate. Ling continues her business in the kitchen. Silence. We hear laughter from the garden followed by a gut-wrenching scream. Ling does not turn around.*)

         (*Lights fade out.*)

第四場

【*燈亮，玲坐在沙發看港產笑片，鮮有的心情愉悅，未幾，Tang與Sammy進，二人相對地神色凝重*】

玲：　　　咦，返嚟嘑？點呀，佢冇咩係嘛？你哋食咗飯未呀？我冇收到D嘢，我冇諗過你哋搞咁耐，不過咁夜，你哋都唔燒架啦？

【*稍頓*】

唔燒我收咗D嘢喇……

TANG：　【*幾乎是自語*】收收收收你老味……

玲：　　　喂，BB聽到喇吓，唔好喺屋企講粗口……

【*見Tang在倒酒*】

你未食飯架？未食飯唔好飲咁多酒。

TANG：　【*沮喪*】你冇嘢嘛？

玲：　　　咩呀？

TANG：　你知唔知發生咩事呀……你有乜理由仲，吓，坐喺度睇周星馳、執埋D……

玲：　　　做咩唧？我知Zoë整親喎，你哋咪送咗佢入醫院囉，我頭先都問佢有冇事架，有事你哋自然會講啦，咁依家佢點吖？係咪辣傷得好嚴重吖？有冇感染到食肉菌吖？冇吖嘛？……D嘢食唔收隔夜會「縮」架！

TANG：　阿Ling，佢半塊面辣傷咗呀！半塊面呀！你知唔知人哋隨時可以告你架？

<u>SCENE 4</u>

(*Lights up. Ling is sitting on the sofa laughing at a Hong Kong film. She is in a good mood. Soon, Tang and Sammy enter. Both look concerned.*)

LING   You're home. So, is she OK? Have you had dinner? I didn't put anything away. I didn't think you'd take this long. But it's so late. You don't want to barbecue anymore, do you? (*Slight pause.*) Then I'll put everything away.

TANG   (*Almost to himself.*) "Then I'll put everything away." Goddamnit.

LING   Do not swear in the house. The baby can hear you. (*Sees Tang pour a drink.*) You haven't had dinner. Don't drink on an empty stomach.

TANG   (*Discouraged.*) Are you insane?

LING   What?

TANG   Don't you know what happened? How can you just…watch Stephen Chow movies and clean up?

LING   What? I know Zoë is hurt. You took her to the hospital. I just asked you if she was all right. If something was wrong, I'm sure you'd tell me. How is she? Is she burnt badly? Is she infected? Is she? …The food will spoil over night!

TANG   Ling, she burnt half her face. Half her face. You know, she could sue you.

玲： 告我？告我咩呀？告我喺佢要求嘅情況下焗熱隻碟等佢枕塊面落去呀？係佢自己興奮得滯咋喎，關我咩事？Sammy, 我有叫你同佢講睇熱架啦！

SAMMY： 係呀，我都有同佢講。

玲： 我邊得閒幫佢隻碟探熱？廚房有咁多嘢做……冇人會放自己塊面落隻碟，咁樣係唔衛生架。

TANG： 你——

玲： 不過佢唔會聽架喇，除非你話係「西」餐廳裡面D「西」人講架啦……

SAMMY： Tang呀，唔好攞嚟嘈啦，唔關崔巧玲事架，冇人估到會發生D咁嘅事架。

TANG： 佢估到，佢知架——我哋第一次同Zoë去Outback食飯佢都係咁，你知道佢會咁，你見過侍應擺隻碟喺佢面前——

玲： 喂，你咁係假設我觀察到呢個行為、記得呢個行為同預測到佢會重複呢個行為，要做好多嘢架，我冇你咁得閒！

SAMMY： 你當崔巧玲係金田一咩，佢冇咁醒架——

玲： 同埋嗰餐飯幾耐之前呀？九個月？年半呀？我冇去記呢D嘢，我根本就唔想記得佢哋嘅嘢。

TANG： 嘩，你認啦？佢認喇！佢唔鍾意Zoë佢哋，佢一開始就睇人唔順眼。

LING   Sue me? Sue me for what? Sue me for heating her plate up at her request so she could put her face on it? She wanted it heated. It's not my fault. I told Sammy to tell her to be careful.

SAMMY   Yeah, I told her.

LING   I didn't have time to check the temperature of the plate. I was busy in the kitchen... Besides, who would put their face on a plate? It's so unsanitary.

TANG   You...

LING   But she won't listen unless you tell her that Westerners in Western restaurants say so.

SAMMY   Tang, don't blame her. It's not Chui Hau Ling's fault. Nobody knew something like this would happen.

TANG   She knew. She did! The first time we went out with Zoë to Outback, we saw the waiter put the plate in front of her face. So you knew she'd do that.

LING   Are you saying that I had observed this behaviour, remembered this behaviour and predicted she would repeat this behaviour? That's a lot of work. I'm quite busy.

SAMMY   You think Chui Hau Ling is Kindaishi? She's not that smart...

LING   And how long ago was that? Nine months? A year and a half? I don't remember that kind of stuff. I don't want to remember that stuff.

TANG   You admit it? She admits it now. She doesn't like Zoë and her husband. She never liked them.

玲: 　呢層我認喎，我係唔鍾意佢哋，但係兩件事嚟，我唔鍾意一個人我可以詛咒佢：望佢身懷巨款喺黑人區蕩失路、望佢返大陸買燕窩又買著豬皮，再唔係娶個民進黨嘅新抱返嚟激死自己，但係除此之外我唔會做任何嘢，我為咩要喺D咁嘅人身上嘥心機！

　　【輕拍肚皮】

　　唔好意思吓BB。

SAMMY: 　咪係囉，BB唔鍾意Daddy Mammy嗌交架……BB呵？BB快D叫Daddy唔好嬲，叫Daddy錫返Mammy……哦，BB話氹人最好係講急口令喎……

玲: 　咩急口令？

SAMMY: 　【*一邊拍手*】鄧家精神，犀利過人——

玲: 　我警告你唔好再重複呢篇嘢吓！次次嚟到呢段我都飛咗佢，哼哼哼，我個仔都踢喇……

TANG: 　……

SAMMY: 　咁呀，猜枚啦：娶公主就娶公主，我話事，我作主

玲: 　呢段都飛……喂，你哋依家香港D電視劇唔得，當D觀眾老人癡呆咁不斷repeat嘅……

　　【*Tang看著二人，仍無動於衷*】

　　……咪咁啦，我哋無謂辛苦張詠兒，人哋咁遠水路嚟到…… 你睇佢面都青晒……

LING   This I do admit. I never liked them. But that's another matter. I can curse people I don't like. I can hope that they get lost in a black neighbourhood with a lot of cash on them. I can hope their leather seats turn out to be vinyl. I can hope their son drives them crazy by marrying a Taiwanese nationalist. But that's all I can do. Why would I bother with these people? (*Pats her stomach.*) Sorry, baby.

SAMMY   That's right. Baby doesn't like mommy and daddy fighting, right, baby? Hey, baby, tell daddy not to be mad. Tell daddy to make up with mommy. Oh, baby said that the best way to make up with someone is to recite tongue twisters.

LING   What tongue twisters?

SAMMY   (*Clapping her hands.*) "Peter Piper picked a peck of pickled peppers, a pack of pickled peppers Peter Piper picked, if Peter Piper --"

LING   I'm warning you. Don't go on. Every time I get to that part I just skip it. Look, my baby is kicking.

SAMMY   Then I'll sing a song "If I could take you to the sky in a rocket…"

LING   Skip that too. Hong Kong soap operas are so bad these days. They think the audience has Alzheimer's. The same storylines, over and over … (*Tang watches them, unmoved.*) Come on. We shouldn't torture Cheung Wing Yee. She came all this way. Look how pale she is…

SAMMY:	係呀,雖然見慣大場面,但係睇住兩公婆開拖真係冇乜經驗──
TANG:	一句講晒,我唔會留喺度……
	【*稍頓*】我唔會留喺屋企幫你湊仔……
玲:	黐線。
TANG:	你就算抄咗我D project趕走晒我D朋友我冇嘢做我都唔會留喺屋企幫你湊細路。我跟本沒諗過係咁。
玲:	我唔會同你討論呢個問題。
TANG:	點解呀?因為有外人喺度呀?
SAMMY:	……其實我可以入房。
TANG:	因為我講中咗哩?你係想抄咗我,你想抄咗我然後我會做你想我做嘅嘢,係,你唔鍾意一個人好簡單,咪唔見佢囉,你不嬲都係咁架啦,你都唔會俾面我應酬佢哋架啦……但係你唔止係咁。你依家開心啦,佢哋唔會再想見到我,因為無論你點講都好,Zoë都認定你係特登,你呢D咁嘅態度係人都睇得出,而且擺到明係因為唔想我同人哋來往。
玲:	咁我講咩都冇用……但係我冇抄咗你D咩,Tang,根本就冇成事過,冇發生過,未發生又點抄咗?
TANG:	係你冇俾佢發生!

SAMMY   Honestly, even though I've been around the block, I'm still not used to husbands and wives fighting.

TANG   Just one thing. I'm not staying here. (*Slight pause.*) I am not staying here to take care of your kid.

LING   Crazy.

TANG   I wouldn't stay home to take care of your kid even if you hadn't sabotaged my projects and kicked out my friends. The idea never even crossed my mind.

LING   I'm not discussing this with you.

TANG   Why? Because we have guests?

SAMMY   …I can go inside.

TANG   Because I hit it on the nose, right? You wanted to sabotage me. You wanted to sabotage my work so I can do only what you want me to do. Yeah. When you don't like someone, it's simple. You just don't see them. That's what you do. You won't even see them for me… But that's not all. Are you happy now? They will never want to see me again because no matter what you say, Zoë will think you did it on purpose. Everybody could see your attitude. It's clear you don't want me to have anything to do with them.

LING   Then I don't need to say anything … But I never sabotaged you, Tang. The deal hadn't gone through, hadn't happened. How can I sabotage something that hasn't happened?

TANG   You made it impossible to happen.

玲: 係你冇俾佢發生！你胸有成竹但係就錯漏百出——你唔係又想話我特登帶明哥嚟抄喎你嘛？Sorry，唔係，我唔知佢哋會上嚟，但就係咁，事實就係咁，求祈搵一個茂利都可以講得出你有幾唔掂，你不如認咗佢啦，咁你會好過一D。

【*Tang離開，靜場*】

玲: 嘖，剩返咁多嘢有排清。

SAMMY: 不如你抖吓吖，我幫你執⋯⋯

玲: 做咩喎，冇嘢喎，兩夫妻總有嗌雲。你睇，仲剩番咁多嘢，難為你喇，呢幾日整個雜錦煲大家食咗佢。唔通掉咗佢咩⋯⋯

SAMMY: ⋯⋯

玲: 唔係連你都以為我特登係嘛？

SAMMY: 唔係，梗係唔係。

玲: 你聽到佢叫我焗暖D架？

SAMMY: 我聽到。

玲: 我有叫你提佢小心辣手。

SAMMY: 我有同佢講。

玲: 咁即係意外啦。

【*靜場，玲忍不住笑*】

你話係咪靚居先？邊有人發花癲發到喺隻碟上面典先⋯⋯

【*Sammy不懂如何反應*】

SAMMY: ⋯⋯希望佢快D好返啦⋯⋯

LING   It was you who made it impossible. You've got a plan but it's full of holes. Are you going to accuse me of bringing Ming here to sabotage your plan? I'm sorry. I didn't know they'd be here. But it happened. Anyone with half a brain could tell you what's wrong with your plan. Why don't you just admit it? You'd feel better.

(*Tang exits. Silence.*)

This is going to take a while to clean up.

SAMMY   Why don't you rest? I'll clean up…

LING   What? Don't worry. Just an ordinary fight between husband and wife. Look at this big pot of rice. Sorry to do this to you but you'll have to share the job of eating it with me for the next few days. We can't just throw it out… You don't think I did it on purpose too, do you?

SAMMY   Of course not.

LING   You heard her asking me to heat it up, right?

SAMMY   Sure.

LING   And I told you to tell her to be careful.

SAMMY   I told her.

LING   So it's an accident. (*Silence. Ling laughs.*) She's nuts. Why would anyone roll her face on a plate?!! (*Sammy doesn't quite know how to react.*)

SAMMY   …I hope she gets well soon…

玲： 有咩吖，辣親吓之嘛。我煮飯成日都辣親架啦，幾日就好返，係佢至叫到咁誇張。

【*稍頓*】

SAMMY： ……對唔住呀崔巧玲。

玲： 做咩講對唔住？

SAMMY： 我唔知你唔想阿Tang做生意。

SAMMY： 唔係，我唔係唔想佢做生意，我係唔想佢群埋嗰堆人啫。你知唔知呢個世界最鍾意搵中國人笨嘅就係中國人，嗰兩個唔係好人嚟架，佢哋唔係真係想搵阿Tang幫佢搞生意，佢哋只不過需要一個阿四……初初識嗰陣三日唔埋兩日就call阿Tang出去問呢問路：邊度開電話卡平啦、邊度買手信好啦，點完阿Tang一輪就俾D小恩小惠佢，咁都算，特登喺阿Tang面前放晒聲氣話自己想搞生意，搞到阿Tang係咁發白日夢。之前已經有單車仔麵，阿Tang嚟咗成擔心機，最後一句唔做咪掟埋一邊，阿Tang失望咗幾耐。

SAMMY： ……我聽佢講因為有人搞咗佢哋至做唔成——

玲： 梗係唔係，係唔想搞總搵到藉口唔搞。估都估到啦，阿Tang又係唔係邊個，人哋無端端做乜出錢俾佢做生意？

SAMMY： 可能阿Tang本事呢，我睇過份proposal，佢都寫得幾好吖……

LING Now what? It's just a small burn. I get burned from cooking all the time. She'll be fine in a few days. Nobody screams like that. (*Slight pause.*)

SAMMY I'm sorry, Chui Hau Ling.

LING Why are you apologizing?

SAMMY I didn't know that you don't want Tang to go into business.

LING It's not that I don't want him to go into business. I just don't want him to hang around those people. There's a lot you don't know. What kind of people take advantage of Chinese people? Other Chinese people! Those two are no good. They don't really want to do business with Tang. They just need a gopher. When we first met them, they'd call Tang every other day for advice. Where do you buy cheap phone cards? Where do you buy good souvenirs? They ask him to do one thing after another and then throw him some crumbs. Fine. But they purposely made him think they wanted to go into business. They got Tang all excited about a fantasy. There was another business idea about a noodle shop. Tang wasted all his time. In the end, they backed out. Tang was disappointed for so long.

SAMMY Tang tells me someone else beat him to it…

LING Of course not. They didn't want to pursue it so they found an excuse not to. You can't blame them. Tang is nobody. Why would anyone give him money to go into business?!

SAMMY Maybe Tang is very capable. I saw his proposal. It's very well written.

玲： 你睇過幾多proposal？你對呢行唔熟對美國又唔熟悉，你覺得好唔代表真係好架。阿Tang有冇本事我唔清楚過你？

SAMMY： ……

玲： 所以我唔鍾意佢哋，佢哋要阿Tang做D自己能力範圍以外嘅嘢，搞到佢自暴其短……你睇過佢份計劃書咩？

SAMMY： 嗯。

玲： 佢幾時俾你睇架？

SAMMY： ……今朝開車出China Town嗰陣。

玲： 黐咗線，佢今次嚟真咁……仲講D咩？

SAMMY： ……冇……淨係好開心咁囉。

玲： 上兩次又係咁，一日廿四小時都喺度提住佢D發達大計——

SAMMY： 佢仲車我落富豪區，然後我哋俾兩個地產經紀夾住嚟遊花園。

玲： 你話佢係咪癲架……唔使講你梗係講咗好多支持嘅說話啦？

SAMMY： 死啦，我係咪俾咗個false hope佢呀？

玲： 【笑】鬼咩，兩個都淨係識發白日夢……

SAMMY： Sorry呀……

LING	You think so? How many proposals have you read? You know nothing about this business and nothing about this country. Just because you think it's good doesn't mean it is. Wouldn't I know better than you how capable Tang is? That's why I don't like them. They want Tang to do things that he's not capable of so he exposes his weaknesses. You saw his proposal?
SAMMY	Mm hmm.
LING	He showed it to you?
SAMMY	…When we were driving to Chinatown.
LING	He's crazy. This time he's really… What else did he say?
SAMMY	…Nothing… Just that he was happy.
LING	It was the same the last couple of times. He's completely obsessed with these get-rich schemes.
SAMMY	He drove me to a rich neighbourhood. We got stuck with some real estate agent who made us go on a tour.
LING	Christ. What the hell was he thinking? You must've given him a lot of encouragement.
SAMMY	Oh no, did I give him false hope?
LING	(*Laughs.*) The two of you. You're both dreamers.
SAMMY	Sorry.

玲:　　　冇咩嘅，佢出去搵朋友飲兩杯就返，佢份人
　　　　冇咩好，勝過D脾氣易嚟易去，搵個人慎兩句
　　　　過咗啖氣就冇嘢。係我慘D，成日俾佢喺背後
　　　　講……我諗佢D朋友一定以為我好乞人憎──
　　　　噴！你睇佢哋幾孤寒，D豬扒咁多肥膏肯定係
　　　　平價貨，快D掉咗佢，一陣食死人……

SAMMY:　　……崔巧玲……你真係想阿Tang留喺屋企湊
　　　　BB？咁樣會唔會嘥咗佢呀？其實你有冇諗過請
　　　　個人返嚟幫手？我聽佢語氣真係好想創一番事
　　　　業咁，佢──

【玲放下手上一切家務，直直地看著Sammy，
頓】

玲:　　　張詠兒，我諗你唔係咁清楚兩個人喺外地生活
　　　　係點。阿Tang個媽咪喺老人院，我屋企人又喺
　　　　晒香港，仲要有乜來往，呢度天大地大我哋冇
　　　　人冇物淨係可以靠對方，如果吓吓都話自己想
　　　　點就點呢個家就唔會成，所以我每個決定都冇
　　　　諗自己鍾意乜而係諗：點樣對屋企利益最大？
　　　　如果今日阿Tang年薪過百萬佢鍾意出去做嘢，
　　　　咪去囉，我而不得喺屋企湊BB，但係現實唔係
　　　　咁，喺我同佢之間我嘅經濟效益大D，咪我出
　　　　去做嘢、佢留喺屋企湊小朋友囉，有乜理由要
　　　　我每個月嘔多千幾蚊美金請個保母返嚟俾佢游
　　　　手好閒？係，呢個就係阿Tang，佢心情好嘅時
　　　　候會諗一堆發達大計、做晒資料搜集好似自己
　　　　係下一屆傑出華人企業家咁，但係唔夠兩日佢
　　　　就會將D計劃書擗埋一邊然後排隊睇Yankee，
　　　　因為佢自己都知自己做唔嚟。其實除咗吹水同
　　　　識整兩杯cocktail阿Tang冇乜特別技能。我咁

LING   It doesn't matter. He's probably out drinking with friends. He's not very capable, but his temper comes and goes quickly. He'll be fine after he talks with someone. I'm the one who suffers. Always talking about me behind my back. His friends must think I'm a witch… Look at how cheap she is. There's so much fat on this pork chop. It must be a cheap cut. This'll kill you. Throw it out.

SAMMY   …Chui Hau Ling…you really want Tang to stay home to take care of the baby? Wouldn't that be a big waste of his ability? Have you thought about hiring someone to help you? I think he really wants to get out there and do something. He… (*Ling stops working and stares at Sammy. Slight pause.*)

LING   Cheung Wing Yee. I don't think you know much about what it's like to live abroad. Tang's mother is in an old folks' home. My family is in Hong Kong and we don't talk much. Out here, with all this space, I have no one to depend on but him. If we do whatever we want whenever we want, this family will collapse. So none of my decisions are based on what I like or don't like. I have to consider what's best for my family. If Tang's annual income was in the millions, of course he could work if he wanted to. And I'd be happy to stay home with the baby. But that's not the case. I am the breadwinner. So I will work, and he will stay home to watch the baby. Why should I spend a few thousand dollars a month to hire a nanny while he does nothing? Yeah, that's Tang. When he feels like it, he'll hatch a dozen get-rich schemes. He'll do all the research like he's some hot shot Chinese entrepreneur. But two days

講唔會特別開心，但係至少我接受呢個事實。再睇開D，好唔好都係自己揀。

所以唔好理佢，我知你一番好意，不過如果真係為佢好，你都係勸佢踏踏實實做人，好多人去到外國都想衣錦還鄉，但係邊個話發達先係成就？可以令一家人好好地咁生活唔係一種成就咩？

SAMMY: 係，梗係。無論喺邊度，可以令一家人好好地咁生活都已經係好大嘅成就。

玲： 咪係囉。但係阿Tang唔明，佢硬係唔肯安守本份……不過佢已經進步咗好多，BB出咗世之後會更加好，佢依家仲未想像到，但係到時有個實物擺喺佢面前，佢見到BB有我哋嘅眼耳口鼻、會喊會笑咁，佢就唔會捨得擺低，呢D係做父母嘅天性，避都避唔㗎，到時佢就會想帶BB去母嬰健康院、去幼稚園，認識其他BB、其他家長，我哋會慢慢建立自己嘅社交圈子，然後真正咁落地生根……

【*玲再次為Sammy扣上衣領*】

玲： 放心啦，好快冇事，遲吓佢心情靚D我叫佢車你落outlet，好多香港人去嗰度買名牌……不過幫我一個忙，聽朝見到佢幫我勸吓佢，唔好成日諗埋D唔等使嘢。你知啦，聽我講得多佢嫌我煩，外人講或者入耳D……

SAMMY: 我明。

later, he'll put his plans aside to watch the NBA, because he knows he's not capable of pulling them off. Actually, besides bullshitting and making cocktails, Tang doesn't have a lot of skills. I'm not happy to say that but at least I accept reality. I have to live with the fact that I chose him. So just let him be. I know you mean well. But if you really want the best for him, get him to be more practical. Everyone who goes abroad wants to return with gold and silver. But how many of us really get rich? Making a comfortable home for the family, isn't that enough of an achievement?

SAMMY   Yes, of course it is. Wherever you are, providing a comfortable home for your family is a huge achievement.

LING   That's right. But Tang doesn't understand that. He refuses to accept his duties… When the baby is born, things will get better. He can't imagine it now. But when it actually arrives, when he sees it has our eyes, ears and nose, that it'll cry and laugh, he won't be able to walk away. That's part of a parent's instinct. You can't avoid it. He'll want to bring the baby to the doctor's or to kindergarten, he'll want to know other babies, other parents. Slowly, we'll build our own social circle, and really start putting down roots… (*Ling buttons Sammy's blouse again.*) Don't worry. Everything will be OK. When he feels better, I'll get him to take you to the outlets. Lots of Hong Kong people shop there for name brands… But do me a favour. When you see him tomorrow morning, talk to him for me. Tell him not to dream up any more crazy schemes. You know how it is. He doesn't want to listen to me. Maybe he'll listen to someone else…

SAMMY   I hear you. (*Lights change.*)

玲：　　　冇嘢架，佢次次都係咁，天光之前就會返。佢
去得邊吖，最多咪揸車出去兜吓風⋯我睇佢今
晚都冇食嘢，等我整定個雜錦煲俾佢先。

LING   Don't worry. He's like this all the time. He'll be home by morning. Where could he go? The most he could do is go for a drive. He didn't eat dinner tonight. I'll make a pot of fried rice and leave it for him. He loves his fried rice…

第五場

【*黑暗中傳來嘔吐聲，強勁音響播放Eminem的"Puke"。*】

【*燈亮，只見Tang抽著大麻。*】

【*Sammy從大門進，將音響停住，Tang動也不動*】

SAMMY: 幾日喇！你去咗邊呀？崔巧玲唔舒服呀！我行嚟行去搵唔到車落downtown，又唔知去邊度剿你！你嗰啲咩嚟架？

TANG: ……你話呢？

【*Sammy欲取，Tang不慌不忙地拿開*】

SAMMY: 俾我！

TANG: 你唔係想食嘅……

SAMMY: 痴線！俾崔巧玲知道鬧死你呀！

TANG: 嘖嘖嘖……變晒，嚟嗰幾日就俾佢茶毒晒……Welcome to the Dark Side……

【*這才發現音樂已停*】做咩熄咗我D音樂呀？唔好聽咩？我特登買嚟送俾阿Ling架，一場夫妻，都有送過乜俾佢，下個月好似係我哋相識週年紀念，我諗住送呢隻碟俾佢，卡都慳返，我淨係用螢光筆highlight咗Puke呢首歌，等佢知道我對呢段婚姻嘅感想——【*唱*】You don't know how sick you make me, you make me

SCENE 5

(In darkness, we hear someone vomiting and loud music playing Eminem's "Puke". Lights up, we see Tang holding a marijuana cigarette. Sammy enters from the front door. Turns off the music. Tang doesn't move.)

SAMMY   It's been days! Where have you been? Chui Hau Ling is sick. I couldn't find a bus downtown. And I didn't know where you went. I… What are you doing?

TANG   What do you think? *(Sammy tries to grab his cigarette but Tang easily evades her.)*

SAMMY   Give it to me.

TANG   Don't you want any?

SAMMY   Give it to me. If Chui Hau Ling found out she'd kill you.

TANG   …You've changed. She's been poisoning you from the day you got here… Welcome to the dark side. *(He realizes that the music has stopped.)* Why did you turn off my music? Don't you like it? I bought it especially for Ling. We're married but I've never given her anything. I think the anniversary of our first meeting is next month. I thought I'd give her this CD. No card necessary. Just use a highlighter to highlight the song "Puke" so she knows how I feel about this marriage. *(Sings)* "You don't know how sick you make me. You make me fucking sick to my stomach…" *(Sammy finally grabs Tang's cigarette and extinguishes it.)* I don't understand fucking sick to my stomach【Sammy終於拿到Tang的煙頭，將它熄滅】……我都唔知你忙D咩……【*Tang冷靜地從西裝袋取出一包大麻，放下CD，若無其事地捲煙*】……我唔驚佢。你驚佢你攞埋林子祥D唱片企出去。我唔驚佢，我坐喺呢度大大聲播Eminem。有冇買旅遊保險？冇買旅遊保險就快D閃，呢度就嚟打仗喇Sammy。

【*Sammy開始收拾四周*】

SAMMY: ……係high好快D high完佢，崔巧玲話今晚早返……

TANG: 你留喺度係嘛？你唔好後悔呀。

SAMMY: ……你睇你！張枱有跡嘞……

TANG: 係咩？咁樣好唔好D？

SAMMY: 小心──你刮花咗喇！有冇搞錯呀！

TANG: ……over over，唯一嘅市民掛住清洗現場唔肯疏散，軍隊可以march in over！

SAMMY: 係呀係呀，到時最緊要睇準D嚟打，唔好傷及無辜添呀！

TANG: 哈……咁你放心，我唔會傷及無辜，我淨係憎佢一個。【*頓*】

SAMMY: Tang，你點可以咁講架，崔巧玲係處理得唔好，但係佢都唔想，呢幾日佢唔見咗你，又唔敢報警，晚晚揸車出去搵你，佢唔舒服都揸車四圍搵你，佢好愛你架，聽到你咁講佢會好傷心──

what you're stressing about. (*Tang calmly takes out a bag of marijuana weed from his suit pocket. He puts down the CD and rolls a joint as if it were nothing.*) I'm not scared of her. If you're scared then grab Alan Tam's CDs and stand outside. I'm not scared. I'm going to sit here and play Eminem. Did you buy travel insurance? You better run if you didn't because war is about to break out, Sammy. (*Sammy begins to tidy up.*)

SAMMY …If you want to get stoned, you better hurry up. Chui Hau Ling said she'd be back early tonight…

TANG You're staying? You may regret it.

SAMMY …Look what you've done. You stained the table…

TANG Really? That's good.

SAMMY Careful. You scratched it. Are you crazy?

TANG Over. Over. Only one civilian here. She is cleaning and refuses to evacuate. The army can march in. Over.

SAMMY Yeah, yeah… When the time comes, aim properly. Don't shoot any innocent bystanders.

TANG Don't worry. I won't hurt the innocent. I only hate her. (*Pause.*)

SAMMY Tang, how can you say that? Chui Hau Ling didn't handle things well, but she didn't do that on purpose. You disappeared for days. She didn't dare call the police so she drove around looking for you. She loves you very much. If she heard you now, she'd be so hurt.

TANG: 佢傷心關我燃事！【*稍頓*】——係喎，屋企唔可以講粗口架呵……但係佢傷心關我燃事？佢愛我關我燃事？你望咩啫你驚佢聽到咩？我好想佢聽到喎！佢依家最好就咴喺我面前，我今次嗌破喉嚨都要佢聽得清清楚楚：我憎你我憎你我好燃憎你！你愛我我唔燃愛你！我好耐之前已經唔燃愛你！我仲日日喺度諗，點解咁多人死唔見你死呀八婆！

【*稍頓*】……痛快，爭D唔記得講粗口係幾咁暢快……更正，應該話爭D唔記得講「真話」係幾咁暢快！不過hold住先，我哋唔好洩咗道氣，唔係一陣唔夠澎湃……我個打火機呢？喺度……嘿嘿……

【*稍頓*】係不斷上升架，我話我憎佢嘅程度，以前滴咗D湯落張枱，佢藐一藐咀，我只係覺得好撚煩，湯之嘛，又唔係溢水，佢好似見到D湯「咋」咁腐蝕緊張枱有煙出緊嚓咁撚樣，都係嗰句：湯之嘛……然後屋企開始有無數咁多規矩，呢個範圍著拖鞋，出到花園著另一對，未沖涼唔准上床，15個item以上至可以開洗碗機……算，跟住埋身呢……譬如話一個本應好地地嘅朝頭早，你著住件乾淨衫想話落唐人街歎返籠點心，佢就同你講今晚開機洗深色衫要你換過件衫去就佢嗰機衫，然後到你換過件深色衫落樓佢已經幫你煎好蛋因為雪櫃D蛋就嚓過期，跟住佢就坐喺你對面同你講一陣陪佢去super買D咩……潔廁劑、洗頭水，除臭丸……個攪拌器壞咗，今個禮拜D士多啤梨減價……經過藥房就入返D喉糖，咖啡唔係buy

TANG I don't give a fuck if she's hurt. (*Slight pause.*) Oh right. I can't swear at home. But I don't give a fuck if she's hurt. I don't give a fuck that she loves me. What are you looking at? Are you worried she'll hear? I want her to hear me. I wish she would appear in front of me right now. This time I am going to tell her everything. I hate you. I hate you. I fucking hate you. You love me but I don't fucking love you. I stopped loving you a fucking long time ago. Every day, I think, so many people die, why don't you die, you bitch! (*Slight pause.*)

That felt great. I almost forgot how wonderful it feels to swear. Correction! I should say, I almost forgot how wonderful it feels to speak the truth. But hold on. Let's not waste our energy now or we won't have enough for later. Where's my lighter? Here it is... (*Slight pause.*)

It never stopped growing. I mean, my hatred for her. She used to make a face if I spilled soup on the table. That just fucking pissed me off. It's soup, for chrissakes, not sulfuric acid. It's like she thought the ingredients were eating right through table, with fucking smoke rising or something. Come on, it's just soup. Then there were all these rules around the house. Wear slippers in this area. Wear something else in the garden. Don't climb into bed without showering. Don't turn on the dishwasher unless there are at least 15 items in there... Fine. Then came the more personal stuff. Like... One fine morning. You put on a clean shirt ready to go to Chinatown for some dim sum. Then she tells you that tonight she's turning on the washing machine one get one free就唔好買……於是，你淨係可以坐喺度冥想，外面風和日麗……

我……我受夠喇……Sammy……我同你講……我真係受夠喇……我已經唔愛佢，無論佢為我做過D乜，我已經唔愛佢……

【*Tang嚎啕大哭，Sammy慢慢坐到他身邊*】

SAMMY: 傻架咩……點會為呢D嘢唔開心成咁架？

【*Tang哭得更厲害*】……唔好揾呢D嘢啦，搞到你亂晒喇——

TANG: 唔好揾我D嘢呀！

SAMMY: 好好好，我唔揾我唔揾……但係Tang呀，好多嘢都可以解決架，你同崔巧玲冷靜D咁傾吓、開心見誠咁傾……可能佢唔知你咁唔開心呢？我係話，佢一定唔知你唔開心成咁……佢呢幾日同我講咗好多你哋啱啱搬入嚟嘅嘢，佢話頭嗰兩日你開心到喺屋企跳嚟跳去……係囉，點解唔試吓諗返D開心嘢啫？剩返D情信呀、結婚相呀咁，呢幾日我睇你哋美國D電視節目都係咁，個counselor入屋幫人fix段婚姻，都係

to wash dark clothes so she tells you to go change. Then after you change and come downstairs, she has fried an egg for you because the eggs in the fridge are almost expired. Then she sits across from you and tells you she wants you to go to the supermarket with her: toilet bowl cleaner, shampoo, mothballs… The blender is broken. The strawberries are on sale this week. Go by the drug store and get some lozenges. Don't buy the coffee unless it's buy one, get one free… So all you can do is just sit there and imagine what a nice day it is outside… I've had enough, Sammy, let me tell ya. I've really had enough. I don't love her anymore. It doesn't matter what she does for me, I don't love her anymore. (*Tang bursts into tears. Sammy slowly moves to his side.*)

SAMMY   Oh, come on, how did things get this bad? (*Tang cries harder.*) Don't touch this stuff. It's making you crazy.

TANG   Don't touch my stuff!

SAMMY   All right, all right, all right, I won't touch it… But Tang, you can work things out. You and Chui Hau Ling just need to calm down and talk openly. Maybe she doesn't know you're so unhappy. I mean, I don't think she knows you're unhappy. She talked a lot these past few days about when you first moved here. She said, for the first couple of days, you were so happy you were jumping all over the house… So, why don't you try and

用呢招……喂我未結過婚都明啦，兩公婆對得太耐，唔記得當初點相愛啫……我唔信你依家對佢一D感覺都冇……

TANG: 有，咪後悔囉。

SAMMY: 咪講埋D晦氣說話啦，你梗係愛崔巧玲先會同佢一齊架？

TANG: 我當時太寂寞……

SAMMY: ……

TANG: ……係……我當時太寂寞……我啱啱去到Chicago，一個朋友都冇……八婆！個八婆乘虛而入！

SAMMY: 一個就算點唔好都跟咗你十年，你都好應該appreciate佢為你付出嘅青春吖——

TANG: 淨係女人先有青春咩？男人都有架！點解佢嗰十年就貴D？我話我三年嘅時間一定貴過佢十年加埋一齊，因為我要俾佢恐嚇、威脅、侮辱——

SAMMY: 對唔住，我聽唔落去，我冇本事，你搵過第二個counselor。

TANG: 你根本乜嘢都唔知！

SAMMY: 你唔抵幫架，都唔係想解決問題嘅！

remember the happy times? Look at your love letters and wedding photos. I've been watching a lot of American TV and it's the same on those shows. The counsellor goes into someone's house to fix their marriage. They do the same thing… I'm not married but even I understand that. A husband and wife forget they love each other because they've been together too long. I can't believe you don't have any feelings for her right now.

TANG   I do. Regret.

SAMMY   Don't be so negative. You must love her to be with her.

TANG   I was lonely then… Yes… I was lonely at the time. I just got to Chicago. I had no friends… That bitch! That bitch took advantage of me.

SAMMY   Tang, you're getting ridiculous… She's been with you for ten years. No matter how bad she is, you can at least appreciate her for giving you her youth.

TANG   You think only women have youth? Men do too. Why are her ten years more precious than mine? Three of my years are more precious than her ten years put together, because she threatens and insults me.

SAMMY   I'm sorry. I can't listen anymore. I can't do this. Find yourself another counsellor.

TANG   You don't know anything!

SAMMY   You don't deserve my help. You don't want to solve the problem.

TANG:	我唔想解決問題？我唔想解決問題就唔會返嚟啦！我今次就係要徹徹底底咁同佢嚟個了斷！

【*不知從哪裡抽出一枝木棍*】

棍我都攞咗枝返嚟呀我話你知！返嚟嗰陣經過個工地見到D人起緊屋，長短粗幼任君選擇，我行過咗架喇，特登掉頭返去揀返枝，本來都有諗住攞架生，但係諗深一層個八婆咁頑強，有備而戰好……等我對準阿Ling個死人頭牛落去，睇吓佢仲有冇咁多嘢講。

【*頓*】

SAMMY:	你唔係真係諗住傷害佢架係咪？
TANG:	……
SAMMY:	喂，阿Tang！
TANG:	……
SAMMY:	你唔係真係會打崔巧玲架係嘛？俾枝棍我。
TANG:	黐線。
SAMMY:	俾我呀！
TANG:	唔俾。
SAMMY:	你唔俾我打九九九架！
TANG:	我幫你打吖，九九九，哎呀，唔通喎……九一一或者有人接嘅。
SAMMY:	你以為我唔敢咩我就打俾你睇……你點可以咁架！諗吓都唔准！你唔好攞D咁嘅嘢嚟講笑！佢有BB架——

TANG I don't want to solve the problem? If I didn't want to solve the problem, I wouldn't have come back! I wanted to come back because I wanted to finish this once and for all. (*He produces a wooden bat out of nowhere.*) I even found myself a wooden bat. When I came back, I passed by a construction site. Long ones, short ones, thick ones, thin ones… you could take your pick. I didn't plan to get any equipment. Then I thought about how strong that bitch is, I better be prepared. I want to take aim and bash her head in. We'll see if she has so much to say then. (*Pause.*)

SAMMY You're not really thinking of hurting her, are you? Hey, Tang? You're not going to hit Chui Hau Ling, right? Give me the bat.

TANG Fuck off.

SAMMY Give it to me.

TANG No!

SAMMY If you won't give it to me, I'll dial 999.

TANG Go ahead. You won't get through. You'll have better luck with 911.

SAMMY You think I wouldn't dare? I'll show you. How can you do this? You can't think like this! Joke about that! For Christ's sake, she's pregnant… (*She takes his phone.*)

TANG I warn you, don't talk to me about that baby. I want to puke when I think about that baby. I want to die every time I think that baby has a 50-50 chance of looking like that bitch.

SAMMY …What are you doing?… What's happening? Why are you doing this? Tang, calm down. This is no big deal…

TANG: 警告你，唔好再攞個BB躂我！我一諗起個B就想作嘔，我一諗起佢有二份一機會似阿Ling個死人樣我就想死！

SAMMY: ……做咩啫……做咩喎……點解要搞到咁……Tang你冷靜D，好小事咋——

TANG: 小事？你話人類嘅尊嚴係小事！你話人類嘅自由係小事——我知你唔會明架Sammy，但係我都要講！我希望呢個世界至少有一個人知，佢——佢想禁錮我。嗰個仆街！佢想禁錮我！

我呢兩日不斷喺度諗，我明明係一個好有目標嘅人，點解會搞到咁？係佢，佢要我留喺呢度，講到所有嘢都為我好咁，其實係唔想我接觸其他人，咁我就可以完全俾佢支配……我終於知道點解佢成日要我將D嘢搬嚟搬去，仲有嗰D字條，佢每一日都會留低好多好多字條叫我做呢樣做嗰樣：鏟泥啦、整屋頂啦、執地牢啦，有時我甚至覺得佢係特登整爛D嘢俾我整……但係點解佢要咁做？我終於諗通咗！佢想搞到我每一日都筋疲力盡，咁我就冇時間諗嘢，咁我就冇時間去諗：其實呢D唔係我想過嘅生活……我只係行錯一步，就要俾佢鎖喺呢間屋！呢段婚姻！呢個身份——你做咩呀！

【Sammy拿走木棍，Tang與之爭奪】

SAMMY:/TANG: 俾我！/唔俾……/放手！/唔好呀！/救命呀！/唔好亂喐！

SAMMY: ——你唔係連我都想打嘛？

【Tang咬了Sammy一口】

SAMMY: 你傻咗呀！做咩咬我呀？

TANG No big deal? Are you saying human dignity is no big deal? Are you saying human freedom is no big deal? I know you don't understand, Sammy, but I have to say this. I wish at least one person in this world would see through her game. She wants to isolate me. That fucking bitch wants to isolate me.

I've been thinking these last couple of days. I used to have purpose. What happened to me? It's her. She wants me to stay here. She says everything she does is for my own good. But in actual fact she doesn't want me to have contact with anyone. Then I can be at her disposal... I finally understand why she keeps telling me to move things here and there. And the notes. She leaves me so many notes every day telling me to do this and that shovel the dirt, fix the roof, clear the basement... Sometimes I think she breaks things intentionally so I have to fix them. But why? I finally figured it out. She wants to exhaust me every day so I have no time to think. So I have no time to think that this is not the life I want... I made one wrong move, and she locked me in this house, this marriage, this identity. What are you doing? (*Sammy has taken the wooden bat and struggles with Tang for it.*)

SAMMY/TANG

Give it to me. / No... /Let go.../Stop it... /Help... /Stop screaming.

SAMMY You want to hurt me too? (*Tang bites Sammy.*) Are you crazy? Why did you bite me?

TANG (*Laughs*) My teeth are itching.

SAMMY That's no reason to bite someone.

TANG:　　【笑】牙痕。

SAMMY:　　牙痕都冇理由咬人架⋯⋯

TANG:　　痛唔痛？

SAMMY:　　試吓我起勢咁咬你一啖睇吓你痛唔痛吖！

TANG:　　⋯⋯

SAMMY:　　好低能呀你——

　　　　　　【Tang強吻Sammy】

　　　　　　【Sammy一棍打著Tang的額頭，Tang隨即大叫】

TANG:　　呀！呀！好痛！好燃痛呀！呀！呀！呀！

　　　　　　【Sammy忽然要再打】

　　　　　　——唔好！唔好打！醒喇！醒晒喇！

SAMMY:　　⋯⋯我話你知你唔好當我流架⋯⋯你試吓⋯⋯你試吓再嚟⋯⋯

TANG:　　知喇⋯⋯仆街⋯⋯好痛⋯⋯

SAMMY:　　你先仆街呀！

TANG:　　我痛咋！我唔係鬧你！

SAMMY:　　我係鬧你！你正仆街！你有幾急呀？吓！美國冇雞叫咩？老婆個friend都搞你係咪人嚟架？！

TANG:　　⋯⋯對唔住呀！我high咗呀⋯⋯我⋯⋯

SAMMY:　　我警告你唔好行過嚟！舉高雙手——shit⋯⋯

　　　　　　【Sammy嚇得掉下木棍，雙手掩眼】

TANG   Does it hurt?

SAMMY   Let me bite you and see if it hurts. You jerk. (*Tang forces a kiss on Sammy. Sammy hits Tang on the head with the wooden bat. Tang screams.*)

TANG   Ow.. That hurts… That fucking hurts… Ow.. Ow.. (*Sammy continues to hit him.*) Stop. Stop hitting me. I'm sober. I'm sober!

SAMMY   Don't underestimate me. If you try that again, if you try to…

TANG   I know! God damn it. That hurts…

SAMMY   Damn you.

TANG   I'm just in pain. I'm not scolding you.

SAMMY   Well, I am scolding you. Damn you. Are you really that horny? Aren't there hookers in America? How can you make a move on your wife's friend? You animal.

TANG   …I'm sorry. I was stoned… I…

SAMMY   Don't you come near me. Put your hands up. Shit… (*Sammy drops the wooden bat from fear. She shields her eyes.*)

TANG   What?

SAMMY   …You… Oh, I'm sick… (*Sammy weakly approaches the sofa.*) You better do something… You're bleeding…

TANG   What? …Hey, you all right?

TANG:	做咩呀？
SAMMY:	……你……我唔得喇……
	【*Sammy虛弱地走向沙發*】
	你快D搞搞佢……你爆缸……
TANG:	吓？……喂，你有嘢嘛？
SAMMY:	……你真係唔好行過嚟……
TANG:	黐線架咩，你以為我仲扯得起咩！
SAMMY:	……唔係呀……我見血暈呀……你唔好俾我見到你……【*二人喘息，Tang隨手拿杯墊擋著自己額頭*】
TANG:	你點呀？使唔使幫你倒杯水呀？
SAMMY:	小心唔好整污糟塊杯墊。
TANG:	得啦，依家仲擔心D咁嘅嘢。
SAMMY:	……唔好再咁喇知嘛？賤人我遇得多，但係你咁樣真係太PK。
TANG:	……起碼我冇乘虛而入吖。
SAMMY:	咁都乘虛而入你就升級做人渣啦。
TANG:	……對唔住。
SAMMY:	算，我當你high咗。
TANG:	……我諗唔完全係——
SAMMY:	你慳D啦，就算幾濫我都有選擇，個對象都唔會係你，你收唔收到！
TANG:	收到。
SAMMY:	又唔諗吓自己係邊個！你以為自己好charm

SAMMY   Don't come near me.

TANG   Oh, c'mon, I'm not horny any more!

SAMMY   …No, I can't stand the sight of blood… Don't let me see you… (*They pant. Tang picks up a coaster and holds it close to his forehead.*)

TANG   How you doing? Want some water?

SAMMY   Don't get blood on the coaster.

TANG   It's fine. Forget the coaster.

SAMMY   …Don't be like that anymore, OK? I've met a lot of jerks, but you take the cake.

TANG   …At least I didn't take advantage of you.

SAMMY   If you did, you'd be scum.

TANG   …Sorry.

SAMMY   Fine. I'll blame it on the drugs.

TANG   …I don't think it's all the drugs.

SAMMY   Shut up. I might sleep around but I can still choose, and I'd never choose you, get it?

TANG   Got it.

SAMMY   You forgot who you were, didn't you? Why did you think I would betray Chui Hau Ling? Cuz you're so charming?

　　　　　　呀？你憑乜嘢以為我會為你出賣崔巧玲——

TANG:　　　OK！唔好再鬧喇得唔得呀？

　　　　　【靜場】

SAMMY:　　……Tang，邊個人冇行差踏錯？我呢世人要
　　　　　後悔嘅嘢，多到數都數唔晒，因為我最叻俾
　　　　　自己一錯再錯……但係你唔同！你有個咁好嘅
　　　　　屋企，你所有嘢都咁好，你錯咗一定要知道點
　　　　　改！唔係有朝一日俾自己行到一個冇彎轉嘅地
　　　　　步……你實後悔。依家仲嚟得切架，聽我講，
　　　　　換個心情，好多嘢可以重新嚟過……我都唔知
　　　　　幾想有呢種機會，我都想所有嘢可以重新開
　　　　　始……【稍頓】

TANG:　　　……你會唔會同阿Ling講？

　　　　　【Sammy搖頭】我唔介意你同佢講，如果可以
　　　　　令所有嘢結束得快D。

SAMMY:　　嘖。你搞到我真係好想食返枝煙……

　　　　　【燈漸暗】

TANG   OK. Get off my case. (*Silence.*)

SAMMY   …You did do me a favour though. At least now I know I still got it… Tang, everyone makes mistakes. I can't even count all the regrets in my life. Because what I'm good at is making one mistake after another. But you're different. You're smart. You learn fast. You have to know how to correct your mistakes. Otherwise, one day, you'll find yourself on a road to nowhere … You'll regret it. You can still make it work, Tang. Listen to me. Change your attitude. Lots of people start over. I only dream of having a chance like this. I'd love to start all over again… (*Slight pause.*)

TANG   …Will you tell Ling? (*Sammy shakes her head.*) I don't mind if you do. Maybe that will make things end sooner.

SAMMY   You're driving me back to smoking.

(*Lights fade out.*)

第六場

【*黃昏，玲拿著幾袋雜物進屋，頓，突然打開大門及所有門窗，Sammy走出來*】

SAMMY: 崔巧玲你返嚟就好喇！阿Tang都啱啱返咗嚟……佢心情好似好返D，我都話啦，佢一定會返嚟，不如你趁呢個機會——

玲: 你喺我屋企食大麻？

SAMMY: ……我——

玲: 你有冇腦架？你知唔知我陀住個細路呀？你喺我屋企食大麻？

SAMMY: 唔係呀崔巧玲——

玲: 你唔使同我解釋，你嘅私生活我無權干預、亦都冇興趣干涉，但係你住得喺度我就希望你識得尊重我。呢度唔係荷蘭食大麻犯法架！而且我一早同你講咗，阿Tang氣管有事，佢聞到煙味會病！幾日啫，你咁都忍唔到？

SAMMY: ……

玲: 點解個個都要令我失望？

【*Tang下樓*】

你做咩呀？

【*玲緊張地走向Tang*】

點解搞成咁呀？

TANG: ……尋晚喺downtown飲完嘢唔覺意撞親個頭。

SCENE 6

(*Dusk. Ling enters the house with a few shopping bags. A moment. Suddenly she opens the front door and all the windows. Sammy enters.*)

SAMMY   Chui Hau Ling, you're home. Tang just got home too… He's not feeling too well. I told you he'd come back. Why don't you try to…

LING   Were you smoking marijuana in my house?

SAMMY   I…

LING   Are you insane? Don't you know I'm pregnant? You smoked marijuana in my house?

SAMMY   No, Chui Hau Ling…

LING   You don't have to explain. I don't care what you do with your life. I'm not even interested. But I hope you'll respect me while you're living under my roof. This is not Holland. Marijuana is illegal. And I told you. Tang has allergies. The smell of smoke makes him sick. It's just for a few days. You can't even control yourself for a few days? Why is everyone disappointing me? (*Tang enters from upstairs.*) What's the matter with you? (*Ling approaches Tang, very concerned.*) What happened?

TANG   …Last night downtown, I hurt myself after a few drinks.

LING   You're so careless! Lemme see.

Tang   Don't touch it.

LING   Does it hurt? Did you use antiseptic before you put the bandage on?

TANG   I said don't touch it.

玲:	咁唔小心嘅！俾我睇吓！
TANG:	唔好搞啦。
玲:	痛唔痛呀？包之前有冇消毒……
TANG:	都話唔好搞咯！
玲:	邊個幫你包架？
TANG:	仲有邊個啫，酒吧入面D人囉。
玲:	鬼佬嚟架？
TANG:	你醒吓啦！係呢間屋先咁多中國人，出面周圍都係鬼佬嚟架！
玲:	鬼佬都用大陸出嘅紗布？D紗布我特登去唐人街買。

【頓，玲打開急救箱將物件重新安放】

TANG:	咁我返到嚟——
玲:	諗清楚先好講，至憎人講大話！
TANG:	依家咩事呀？係咪一返嚟就要撩交嗌呀？
玲:	我由頭到尾都同你講緊道理。
TANG:	我喺屋企整親咁得未呀！
玲:	喺屋企整親點解唔可以照直講呢？
SAMMY:	Ok，Sorry崔巧玲，其實係我唔小心整親佢……阿Tang驚我唔好意思所以話佢自己整親……你哋唔好嗌交啦。

LING   Who put it on for you?

TANG   Who else? People in the bar.

LING   Westerners?

TANG   Wake up! Everyone outside is a Westerner. The only Chinese people are here in this house.

LING   Since when do Westerners use gauze from China? I bought this in Chinatown. You can't get it anywhere else. (*Pause. Ling opens the first aid kit and rearranges the contents inside.*)

TANG   Well…

LING   Think before you speak. I hate it when people lie.

TANG   What's the matter with you? Why are you picking a fight?

LING   I'm just trying to get at the truth.

TANG   I hurt myself here at home. OK?

LING   If that's true, then why did you have to lie.

SAMMY   Sorry, Chui Hau Ling. Actually, I was careless and hurt Tang… He's just trying to save me embarrassment so he said he hurt himself… Please don't fight.

LING   You hurt him? How did it happen?

玲: 你整親佢？點發生架？

SAMMY: 你哋呢度好靜⋯⋯我自己留喺屋企又好驚⋯⋯佢入屋嗰陣我以為係賊所以嚟手攞咗D嘢扑佢——

玲: THIS IS BULL SHIT!

SAMMY: 當時我high咗。Sorry。

【頓】

玲: 我都估到。真架。我一早估到⋯⋯有嘢架，咁你依家知道後果，呢D嘢唔止傷害你仲會傷害到你身邊嘅人。有時唔係淨係自己開心就得架，都要為人設想——

TANG: 夠喇！好少事咋！意外嚟架OK？【玲提著急救箱走到Tang旁，想為他重新包紮】做咩啫！

玲: 我肯定你冇洗過個傷口。

TANG: 唔洗呀！

玲: 唔洗會發炎架——

TANG: 咁我自己洗得未呀！

玲: 是但你。

【玲進房】

TANG: 對唔住——

SAMMY: 【一邊扣上衣領】算啦唔好再講——

TANG: 佢係咁架——

SAMMY: 是但啦。有咩等我走咗先搞，我唔該你，我唔想involved。【玲出】

SAMMY   It's so quiet here… I was a little scared to be alone … So when he came in , I thought he was a thief and hit him over the head…

LING   THIS IS BULLSHIT!

SAMMY   I was stoned! Sorry. (*Pause.*)

LING   I knew it. Really. I always knew it. Now you see what that stuff does. It hurts not only you, but those around you. Sometimes you have to be more considerate and not just think about your own pleasure.

TANG   That's enough. It's nothing. It was an accident, OK? (*Ling brings the first aid kit over to Tang and starts to redress his wound.*) What are you doing?

LING   I'm sure you didn't wash the wound.

TANG   Forget it.

LING   It'll get infected.

TANG   I'll wash it myself.

LING   Fine. (*Ling exits to her room.*)

TANG   I'm sorry.

SAMMY   (*Buttons her shirt.*) Forget it.

TANG   She's like that…

SAMMY   I don't care. Whatever you want to do with her, just wait till I've left. Please, I don't want to be involved. (*Ling enters.*)

玲: 今晚唔煮飯，買咗Take away。

SAMMY: ⋯⋯我唔肚餓，你哋食先吖──

玲: D嘢翻熱冇益，食咗先啦。

【*很長的沈默，只聽到刀叉碰撞、桌椅移動等準備晚餐的聲音*】

【*最後三人終於都坐在餐桌前，進食，靜場*】

SAMMY: 其實Chinese take away都ok吖，我聽D人講呢D係俾鬼佬食嘅唐餐，但係我覺得都幾好食呀。

TANG: ⋯⋯

SAMMY: 差D唔記得fortune cookie！今日運程係：Love and you shall be loved⋯⋯都唔係講fortune嘅⋯⋯崔巧玲我幫你睇下──

玲: 唔使喇，我唔信呢D嘢。

【*又一陣沈默*】

SAMMY: ⋯⋯係呀⋯⋯我斗零都冇，後日要麻煩你哋車我去機場喇！

TANG: 其實你鍾意可以住多幾日。

SAMMY: 唔喇，我都係想早D番去，再請假俾公司炒。

TANG: ⋯⋯

SAMMY: 遲吓BB出世記住映相返嚟俾我睇。

玲: 係喇，明哥今日打電話嚟問起你。

SAMMY: 明哥？

玲: 嗰日上嚟嗰個阿明呀，咁快就唔記得嘑。

SAMMY: ⋯⋯記得⋯⋯佢做咩問起我？

LING   I didn't cook tonight. I bought take-out.

SAMMY   …I'm not hungry. You go ahead.

LING   It's not very nutritious if you reheat it. Just eat it now. (*A long silence. All we hear is the noise of utensils, the moving of furniture and other noises of preparing dinner. Finally, all three are seated at the table to eat, in silence.*)

SAMMY   …Oh right… I have no money. Could you please drive me to the airport the day after tomorrow?

TANG   You don't want to stay a few more days?

SAMMY   No, thanks. I want to go back. If I take anymore time off, they'll fire me. When the baby is born, send me photos. (*Another moment of silence.*) Actually the Chinese take-out is OK. I hear Chinese people say that this is the kind of Chinese food Westerners eat. But I think it's quite good. Oh, I almost forgot. My fortune cookie. It says, "Love and you shall be loved". That's not a fortune... Tang, what does yours say? Chui Hau Ling, let me see yours …

LING   By the way, Ming called and asked about you today.

SAMMY   Ming?

LING   He was here the other day. Don't you remember?

玲：　你真係奇怪，你叫我介紹男人俾你識架嘛，咁你哋見過面，人哋咪問起你囉。

SAMMY：　……咁你幫我問候返佢吖。

玲：　你覺得佢點呀？

SAMMY：　幾好吖——不過我覺得佢好似彭嘉龍！我第一眼就覺得佢似，彭嘉龍係我哋以前街口士多舖老板個仔，讀書好叻架，最鍾意叫崔巧玲買佢哋舖頭D唥唥冰請佢食，好無賴，佢仲會失驚無神掉舊擦膠入口嚼到碎晒然後lur返出嚟，明哥個樣好似佢。

TANG：　你哋嗰個彭嘉龍又係碌葛咁架？

SAMMY：　【笑】……咁架你！崔巧玲呀！你老公把口好衰呀……

玲：　【看著Sammy】吖，我發覺你每次唔想答一D問題嘅時候就會講笑架喎。

SAMMY：　……

玲：　講真架，你覺得啱唔啱？

SAMMY：　你意思係男女關係嗰種？

玲：　唔通兄妹關係嗰種咩。

SAMMY：　……Sorry，我冇諗過。

TANG：　唔啱你直接講，你唔使講任何嘢嚟滿足佢——

SAMMY：　其實明哥都幾好架！真架，嗰晚我同佢傾咗兩句，佢心地好好，人又老實……不過唔知呢，相處嘅時間唔多，我冇乜感覺。

SAMMY   I remember… Why was he asking about me?

LING   You're something. You asked me to introduce you to someone. Now you've met him. That's why he asks about you.

SAMMY   Then please send my regards.

LING   What do you think about him?

SAMMY   He's nice… But I think he looks like Pang Ka Lung. The moment I laid eyes on him I thought of that. Pang Ka Lung was the son of the owner of that store on our street. He was a great student. He always used to ask Chui Hau Ling to give him popsicles from his dad's store. What a rascal. He used to put an eraser in his mouth, chew it up, then spit it out for no reason. Ming looks like him.

TANG   Was Pang Ka Lung also socially inept?

SAMMY   (*Laughs.*) That's terrible. Chui Hau Ling. Your husband's so bad…

LING   (*Looks at Sammy.*) Every time you want to avoid answering a question you make a joke. Do you realize that? Stop ducking my question.

SAMMY   You're asking about relationships?

LING   I'm certainly not asking about the price of tea.

SAMMY   …Sorry. I didn't realize.

TANG   You don't have to say what she wants to hear. Just say what's on your mind.

SAMMY   Actually, Ming is OK. Really. I talked a little with him that night. He seems really nice. And honest… but, I don't know. We haven't known each other long. I don't have any feelings for him.

玲：　　　右辦法啦，中途殺出兩個無謂人。

【*Tang走向酒吧添酒*】

我哋唔係講好咗晚飯嘅時候淨係飲一杯咩？

TANG：　由今日開始我鍾意飲幾多杯鍾意幾時飲由我自己話事！

SAMMY：崔巧玲呀——

玲：　　　頭先講到咩話——呀感覺，感覺呢D嘢可以培養嘅。

TANG：　睇吓同邊個啦。

玲：　　　你想唔想走之前再搵個時間約佢出嚟吖？

SAMMY：崔巧玲其實唔使喇，我諗我同佢應該唔係好work——

玲：　　　你唔鍾意佢D乜？佢唔靚仔？個人唔夠風趣？右嘢架，純粹討論層面，頭先你至話佢老實，我都覺得佢做嘢好勤力——

TANG：　咁嫁隻牛都得啦。

玲：　　　都有D似架，但係咁又有咩唔好呀？老實同勤力幾時變成一種缺點？起碼佢自力更生，自己供緊一間屋仲寄錢去台灣供佢細佬妹讀書！就算佢係一隻牛我哋都應該尊重佢！【*Tang一口喝盡，生氣地倒另一杯*】【*玲二話不說從櫃中取出一枝最貴的酒，拔去酒塞，在洗手盆傾盡*】

【*長停頓，玲復坐原位*】不如我哋傾吓擇偶條件——【*Tang進入花園*】其實你想要一個點樣嘅人？背景係點？咩國籍、邊類性格諸如此類，你有冇諗法？

LING	Well, we had some very rude intruders. It couldn't be helped. (*Tang goes to the bar for another drink.*) Didn't we agree that we only have one drink at dinner?
TANG	From now on, I will decide how many drinks I have and when I want to have them.
SAMMY	Chui Hau Ling…
LING	Where were we? Oh yes, feelings. Feelings can be nurtured.
TANG	It depends with whom.
LING	Do you want to see him again before you leave?
SAMMY	I don't think so. I don't think it's going to work out between us.
LING	What don't you like about him? Not good looking enough? Not fun enough? That's just superficial stuff. You said he is honest. I think he is very hard working…
TANG	Then marry a cow.
LING	He does seem like one but what's wrong with that? When did honesty and hard work become flaws? At least he works. He has a mortgage and he sends money back to Taiwan for his younger brothers' and sisters' tuition. We have to respect him even if he is a cow. (*Tang downs his drink and angrily fixes another one. Ling says nothing, approaches a cupboard, brings out the most expensive bottle, uncorks it and pours the contents into the kitchen sink. Long silence. Ling returns to her seat.*) Let's talk about the requirements of a mate. (*Tang exits into garden.*) What are you looking for in a man? What kind of background? What nationality or personality? What do you think?

SAMMY: ……我……冇……

玲: 你冇諗法？定係你心有所屬？諗住返香港之後點？Ok搬咗屋轉咗工換埋電話號碼咁下半世呢？唔通日日望天打掛，睇吓個天幾時跌第三個李嘉誠俾你？

SAMMY: ……崔巧玲……點解你今晚好似……你有D怪……如果係因為隊草嗰件事，我可以解釋架……定係我做錯D乜——

【Tang從花園進來，揪住一大束剛剪下的鮮花】

【玲怔怔地看著Tang將其中一朵插在Sammy頭上，Sammy呆住了】

玲: 你咁樣係乜意思？

TANG: 等你知道失去心愛嘅嘢感受係點。

玲: D酒係我用錢買。

TANG: D花係我做到隻狗咁種佢出嚟。

玲: 你係咪決定以後都用咁嘅態度對我？

TANG: 係，我決定以後都咁對你。

玲: 就係因為佢？

TANG: 唔完全係。

玲: 你識咗佢幾耐呀？

TANG: 我唔理，總之同佢道歉。

玲: 點解要我道歉呢？

TANG: 因為你乞人憎，一入屋就呫住人，人哋走都走唔切，你feel唔到架咩？

SAMMY   …I… haven't thought…

LING   You haven't? Or have you already found someone? What will you do after you return to Hong Kong? So you've moved, gotten a new job and changed your phone number, now what? Just wait? See when the third Li Ka Shing will show up?

SAMMY   …Chui Hau Ling… you seem very… you seem kind of strange tonight. If you're upset because I smoked pot, I can explain… Or have I done something wrong? (*Tang enters from garden with a bunch of fresh cut flowers. Ling watches Tang put a flower on Sammy's head. Sammy freezes.*)

LING   What the hell are you doing?

TANG   Now you know what it feels like to lose something you love.

LING   I paid for the wine.

TANG   I slaved like a dog to plant the flowers.

LING   Are you going to treat me like this for the rest of your life?

TANG   Yes, I'm going to treat you like this for the rest of my life.

LING   Because of her?

TANG   Not entirely.

LING   How long have you known her?

TANG   I don't care. Apologize to her.

LING   Why should I?

TANG   Because you're a bitch. You've been on her case since the moment she arrived. She can't wait to leave here. Can't you see that?

SAMMY: Tang，唔關你事呀！

玲: 你係純粹想幫人出頭吖定唔捨得佢……我唔會同佢道歉，佢同我道歉就差唔多，一路呃住我。

SAMMY: 咩呀？崔巧玲，你講咩呀？

玲: 咩事？你瞞住我，又話業主加租、又話自己想轉工、好耐冇拍拖咁……原來你同你老細攪埋一齊，有婦之夫㗎架，搞到人哋個老婆跳樓自殺，知情嘅人都杯葛佢，於是佢未自動辭職囉，但係成個圈子有幾大？稍為要面嘅都搵工轉啦。係咪奇怪點會傳到嚟呢度？【*將一包裹扔在桌上*】我寄俾你D旅遊資料，退返公司，裡面有封影印信，寫晒你D嘢──人哋老婆D屋企人擺明要佢臭名遠播，你自己睇，印埋你張相，我諗寄過信去你舊屋嘅人都會收到呢張嘢。

SAMMY: ……

玲: 呀，爭D唔記得話俾你知，今日收到呢份嘢之後我上過你個blog，你呢排唔睇佢啦架，唔係你一定心都寒，上面鬧你D留言真係多到呢……

SAMMY: OK，夠喇。我係做錯嘢，但係唔係你諗咁樣……我同Alvin喺佢老婆自殺之前已經分咗手──

SAMMY   Tang, it's not about you.

LING   Are you sticking up for her or don't you want her to leave? I won't apologize to her. She should apologize to me. She's been lying to me.

SAMMY   What are you talking about?

LING   You lied to me. You said your landlord raised your rent, you want to get a new job, it's been a while since you dated... You had an affair with your boss. He's married. His wife jumped off the roof. People who knew started shunning you so you had to quit your job. But the community is very small. Anyone with any dignity would have quit. You must be wondering how the news travelled all the way over here to me. (*Takes out a package and throws it on the table.*) The package of sightseeing information I sent you got returned to my office. Along with a photocopy of a letter that talks all about you. The dead wife's family is determined to spread the news everywhere. Look at yourself. There's your photo. I think anyone who sent mail to your old address would've received one. Oh, I almost forgot. I went on your blog after I got this today. It's a good thing you haven't read it for a while. You'd be mortified. You should see the number of devastating messages people have left for you.

SAMMY   That's enough. I made a mistake. But it wasn't what you think... Alvin and I broke up before his wife committed suicide.

玲: 呢層我知吖，網上面都有講，話你利用完人、攞到D甜頭之後就飛起人吖嘛。但係你老細就用情太深，想用離婚去挽救呢段婚外情——網上面寫得好仔細，直頭好似睇連載小説咁，只係冇乜驚喜。

SAMMY: ……點解你要咁樣對我？點解你可以咁殘忍？你根本冇諗過我面對緊乜嘢。Alvin喺我媽咪過身嗰陣出現，我哋已經一齊好多年，我真心愛佢架……你以為我冇走過？你以為我從來冇掙扎過？我有為我嘅懦弱付出代價架，點解你要揀呢個時候comment我？

玲: 錯，我冇comment你，我話知你推佢老婆落樓。我只係嬲。我做好心，勸你喺度搵個人嫁咗佢費你返香港受難，呢個懵丙就喺度懶醒，懶叻咁喺度同我搞對抗，做咩啫，插朵花喺度代表咩？你接手呀？

SAMMY: OK！就算我點衰我搞過人哋老公都唔代表我會——我知自己有底線……係，可能我唔應該瞞你，但係我唔會向你道歉，我點解唔可以選擇開開心心咁做個過客——

玲: 因為我有權知囉。因為我打開個門口俾你入嚟。因為我要知道自己係唔係引狼入室。

SAMMY: 咩引狼入室啫？我知你依家好嬲……但係你可唔可以信我？我哋識咗咁耐，如果連你都唔信我——

玲: 我問你，你哋兩個之間究竟發生過D乜？有D乜嘢係我應該知又未知呢？【頓】

LING	I know that. It's all there on the Internet. It talks about how you used and took advantage of him, then blew him off afterwards. But your boss was too far gone. He hoped to get you back by divorcing his wife… It's all very well documented on the Internet. It reads like an epic novel. Except that it's so predictable.
SAMMY	Why are you doing this to me? How can you be so cruel? You don't know what I had to deal with. Alvin appeared when my mother passed away. We had been together many years. I really loved him. Don't you think I tried to leave him? Don't you think I fought this? I've paid for my weakness. Why are you judging me now?
LING	I'm not judging you. I don't care if you pushed his wife off the roof. I'm just mad. I thought I was being nice, telling you to find a nice husband so you don't have to go back to Hong Kong and deal with all this. This loser here is such a genius. He thinks he's pushing my buttons. What is the meaning of this? What's with the flowers?
SAMMY	I know I had an affair with a married man. But that doesn't mean I would… I know where to draw the line… True, I shouldn't have lied to you. But I won't apologize. Why can't I just be a happy tourist?
LING	Because I had a right to know. I opened my door to you. I should know if I've invited a wolf into my home.
SAMMY	Wolf? I know you're mad right now, but how can you not trust me? We've known each other for so long. If you don't believe me then…
LING	Tell me. What happened between the two of you? What should I know that I still don't know? (*Pause.*)

SAMMY: 我最後一次答你：冇。【頓】

TANG: 有又點呀？

SAMMY: ……你講咩呀？！

TANG: 我問你有又點呀？你可以點啫？

SAMMY: 你唔好亂噏呀！

TANG: 今日晏晝佢摷我隊草，我哋就喺呢張梳化搞咗。/ 你可以點吖？都話咗你，大住個肚就唔好請D姊妹上嚟 / 唔係，其實我係你嘅話冇大肚都唔會請女仔friend上嚟 / 要索過你唔係好難咋。

SAMMY: 【幾乎是撲向Tang】仆街！/ 你講乜嘢呀！/ 你黐綫架！/ 佢黐綫架！

玲: ……

SAMMY: 崔巧玲——

玲: 你同我收聲。執包袱。走。我聽到你把聲就憎。返去你自己嘅地方。我唔使嘥氣鬧你。香港大把人等緊你。

SAMMY: ……我會走，我一定走……但係我哋可唔可以唔好咁樣講再見……崔巧玲你唔係真係信佢講嘅嘢嘛……OK……如果你覺得香港嗰件事你有權知，我同你道歉……係我自私……我唔想你好似其他人咁judge我……但係呢段日子我都唔好過架崔巧玲……我日日望住個電話唔知可以打俾邊個，然後你覆我e-mail話你有咗，我覺得呢個世界好似突然有返D希望……我以為我可以分享到你嘅開心……我係衷心嚟祝福你……【Sammy決定離開】

SAMMY   I will say it one more time – nothing! (*Pause.*)

TANG   What if something did happen?

SAMMY   What are you doing?

TANG   I said, what if something did happen? What would you do about it?

SAMMY   Shut up!

TANG   This afternoon she offered me pot. We had sex on the sofa. What are you gonna do about it? I told you not to invite your friends over when you're this pregnant. No, actually, if I were you, I wouldn't invite friends over even if you weren't pregnant. Any woman is better than you.

SAMMY   (*Almost charging at Tang*) Fuck you. What are you saying? Are you insane? You're crazy. Chui Hau Ling?

LING   Shut up. Pack your bags and get out. I hate the sound of your voice. Go back to where you came from. Lots of people there would love to get their hands on you. I don't have to waste my energy.

SAMMY   …I'll leave… I will. But do we have to part like this? Chui Hau Ling, you don't believe him, do you? OK, if you think you have the right to know what happened in Hong Kong, I'm sorry. I was selfish. I didn't want you to judge me like other people. But it was really painful for me too… Every day, I'd stare at the phone not knowing who I could call. When you sent me an email telling me that you were pregnant, I felt like there was some hope in this world. …I thought I could feel happiness through you. I honestly wish you well… (*Sammy decides to leave.*)

TANG: 唔好走。【*Tang攔著她*】

唔准走!

SAMMY: 你仲想點?

TANG: 點解你要走?點解你唔鬧返佢?你唔使俾佢咁鬧。我都唔使俾佢咁鬧。

玲: Tang,容忍有個限度,我諗你唔記得,你係唔可以冇咗我。

TANG: No!我係可以冇咗你!我決定搏一舖。還掂出到去又係坐監,喺呢度同坐監都冇乜分別——

【*Tang拉住Sammy*】

SAMMY: 放手……放手!你哋兩個係咪有病架!

TANG: ……做咩唧,你都見到佢幾乞人憎啦?呢個係你唯一可以反擊嘅機會!Ok,不如我咁講,其實你唔係真係咁了瞭解佢,佢頭先咪鬧到你狗血淋頭嘅?我同你講佢冇資格!佢都有好多嘢都冇話俾你知……依家好喇,既然你返去要受靶,不如留喺度——

SAMMY: 我做咩要留喺度?

TANG: 重新開始囉!我終於明白點解你成日話想重新開始!Sammy!一D都唔遲架!我同你都仲有機會!【*頓*】

玲: 吖,我真係冇諗過呢個可能性。

TANG: 冇諗過哩,我終於有D諗法係impress你喇係嘛?【*頓*】

玲: 你諗住點同我公司D人交代?

TANG   Don't go. (*Tang blocks her way.*) You can't leave.

SAMMY   What do you want?

TANG   Why should you leave? Why don't you tell her off? You don't have to stand here and take it from her. I don't have to either.

LING   Tang, there are limits to my patience. I think you've forgotten that you can't live without me.

TANG   No, I can. I've decided to take a chance. I'm going to jail if I leave this place. That's no different than living here. (*Tang grabs onto Sammy.*)

LING   Don't touch her in front me.

SAMMY   Let go… Let go… You're both sick.

TANG   What? You see how damn annoying she is. This is your only chance to get back at her. Actually, I should say, you really don't know her very well. Just now she was telling you off. She has no right, believe me. There's a lot she hasn't told you about herself too… This is perfect. If you have to return to face your punishment, then just stay here…

SAMMY   Why would I want to stay here?

TANG   To start again. I finally understand why you keep talking about starting again. It's not too late, Sammy. We still have a chance. (*Pause.*)

LING   That is not possible.

TANG   No? Have I finally found a way to impress you? (*Pause.*)

LING   What will you tell people at my office?

TANG: 你真係勤力，一諗就諗做嘢先——我咪同佢哋講你老豆喺香港就嚟死，趕住返去。

玲: 然後就話我決定留喺香港。

TANG: 要打理家族生意，whatever。你班手下一定開心到發癲。

玲: 咁母嬰健康院嗰邊呢？

TANG: 上網幫你改appointment。遲D通知佢哋你轉去另一間。

玲: 錢嗰方面點解決？

TANG: 做返bartender，還掂間屋已經供斷。

玲: 咁你個哎呀阿媽呢？

TANG: 我諗過喇，大不了接佢返嚟住。佢都唔會認得我。

【稍頓】

玲: 我想知道，你呢個諗法究竟盤算咗幾耐？

TANG: 耐到你唔信。

SAMMY: 你哋講緊咩？

TANG: 阿Ling開始有Dejavu。

玲: 我勸你唔好講，唔講仲有得返轉頭。

TANG	You're amazing. Always so practical. I'd tell them your father died in Hong Kong and you had to leave immediately.
LING	And then, that I decided to stay there.
TANG	To take care of family business…whatever. Your staff would be ecstatic.
LING	What about the pre-natal clinic?
TANG	I'd change your appointment online. Then tell them later that you went to another clinic.
LING	What about money?
TANG	I could bartend again. The mortgage on the house is paid off.
LING	What about your so-called mother?
TANG	I thought about that. If worse comes to worse, she could live here. She doesn't recognize me anyway. (*Slight pause.*)
LING	Tell me, how long have you been hatching this plan?
TANG	You have no idea.
SAMMY	What are you talking about?
TANG	Ling is experiencing déjà vu.
LING	You'd better not say anymore. If you don't say it, you can still go back.

TANG: 你點會以為我仲想返轉頭？

Sammy你坐低，講件事你知吖——你記唔記得自己話過，邊個人冇行差踏錯？你講得啱，好多人都有做錯，分別只係有D人會被揭發，而有D人就要等天譴……十年前喺Chicago，有個留學生因為太想脫離屋企，衝動之下嫁咗俾一個當地華僑。婚後佢相當後悔，因為佢發現自己根本唔愛呢個男人，於是乎佢背住老公同一個bartender搭上……佢哋愈搞愈認真，個老婆就遊說自己嘅老公搬去另一個省、一個偏僻好多嘅地方，本來只係為咗避人耳目，但係就喺佢哋啱啱搬嗽San José嘅時候，有一次喺新屋鬼混嗰陣俾個老公撞破，個女人錯手殺死咗佢老公……

玲: 係個姦夫錯手殺人。

TANG: 係個女人錯手殺人！不過佢當時好冷靜！所以令個姦夫相信殺人嗰個係自己！呢個女人好似乜都預計好晒，首先用最可怕嘅結果嚟恐嚇呢個姦夫，然後喺佢面前展開一個唔知幾耐之前就擬定好嘅計劃：佢話佢老公冇乜親戚，只有一個患咗老人癡呆症嘅媽媽；佢話佢哋啱啱搬嗽San José，冇乜人知道呢度嘅新地址；佢話佢知道老公所有嘅密碼，所有嘢都可以through電腦調動。最後，佢攞住佢老公張駕駛執照同

TANG	Why would you think I'd want to go back? (*Tang forces Sammy to take the wooden bat.*) Sammy, sit down. I have to tell you something. Do you remember saying that everyone makes mistakes? You're right. Everyone makes mistakes. The difference is, some people's mistakes are discovered, and some people will have to be punished by god. Ten years ago in Chicago, a student from abroad hastily married a local Chinese man because she wanted to leave home. She regretted her marriage because she discovered that she didn't love this man. So she started to have an affair with a bartender behind her husband's back. They got very serious. The wife talked the husband into moving to another state, to a very remote area, so no one would find out about the affair. But one time soon after they moved to San José, the husband walked in on the adulterous couple and the woman killed the husband by accident...
LING	The man killed the husband.
TANG	The woman killed the husband! But she was cool! And she made the man believe he was the one who killed him! It was like she had the whole thing planned. First, she came up with the cruellest ways to threaten the man. Then she presented him with a plan that she'd been hatching for god knows how long. She said her husband had no family, just a mother with Alzheimer's. She said they just moved to San José and no one had their new address. She said she knew all her husband's passwords. She could move things around on the computer. Finally, she showed me her husband's driver's license and said, "This is America. Get a

我講，呢度係美國，你晒黑D，加返副眼鏡，冇人會睇得出兩個中國人嘅分別，只要你一世唔出國，呢個身份永遠都屬於你⋯⋯

SAMMY: ⋯⋯

TANG: 個姦夫就順理成章咁做咗佢老公。但係為咗避免東窗事發，呢對夫婦幾乎係切斷晒以往嘅人際關係——

根住落嚟發生乜你都知架！個假老公好可憐，佢幾乎俾呢個女人支配住，雖然一路冇人發現，但係佢做乜都冇晒自由，因為個女人總係用呢樣嘢要脅住佢⋯⋯

SAMMY: 點解你要話俾我知⋯⋯

玲: 因為佢想換你做女主角。

TANG: 係work架Sammy！係work架！咁耐以嚟都冇事⋯⋯你剪吓個頭、換過D衫——

玲: 不過都要搞一輪嘢囉，譬如話，你要整死我先。

SAMMY: 阿Tang你唔會真係做得出嘅！

玲: 佢做得出，佢點做唔出呀，你冇睇佢叉住我前夫條頸嗰個樣——

TANG: 係你搲床頭燈扑濕佢先架，嗰三吓「Kong、Kong、Kong」我到依家發夢都聽到呀！

玲: 咁係咪你撞佢隻眼埋枱角？係咪你踢斷佢肋骨？係咪你沿住條木樓梯拖佢落嚟？係咪你明知佢未斷氣都壅第一堆泥上去——咁係咪你殺人呀？！

suntan. Put on a pair of glasses and no one will know the difference between two Chinese men. As long as you don't leave the country, you can have this identity forever." So the adulterous man became her husband. But to avoid being discovered, the couple almost completely cut themselves off from all their previous relationships. And you know what happened after that. The poor fake husband became completely dominated by the woman. Although they were never discovered, he lost all his freedom because that's what she threatened him with…

SAMMY   Why are you telling me this?

LING   Because he wants to find another female lead for this show. (*Sammy wants to run but is captured.*)

TANG   It will work, Sammy. It will. It's worked all this time… Cut your hair, change your clothes…

LING   You'd have to do something else first, like, kill me.

SAMMY   Tang would never do that!

LING   He would. He can do it. You didn't see how he strangled my dead husband's neck.

TANG   You smashed a lamp over his head first. That sound, "Kong… Kong… Kong…" I still hear it in my dreams.

LING   Didn't you push his eye against the corner of a table? Didn't your kick break his ribs? Didn't you push him down the stairs? Didn't you dump the first shovelful of dirt over him while he was choking? Didn't you kill him?

TANG:	你收聲！

【*Sammy想逃跑卻又被截回*】

TANG:	Sammy！佢唔係好人嚟架！攞住枝棍！
SAMMY:	我唔要！放我走！
TANG:	我發誓！我一定唔會好似佢對我咁對你……
SAMMY:	求吓你放我走……
TANG:	你唔使驚！我會幫你架！
SAMMY:	放我走——
TANG:	點解啫！你都話鍾意呢邊嘅生活！
SAMMY:	但係我唔想同你一齊！我唔想同你有任何瓜葛！【*頓*】……我連你係邊個都唔知。

【*頓，Sammy退到一角，玲難過地坐在一旁*】

TANG:	……我係邊個都唔重要，你冇得揀，因為你已經知道呢件事。我係嚟真架，我真係嚟真架，我今次真係嚟真架。一係你，一係阿Ling，會長埋喺阿Tang隔離。

唔使諗住反抗，你快唔過我，反抗即係迫我做決定，我最怕咁急做決定……我哋唔需要相愛架Sammy……我哋甚至可以有各自嘅生活……我哋只需要住喺呢間屋，令所有嘢如常運作……【*Tang半推著Sammy走向玲*】

首先你要燒咗本passport……証明你唔會偷偷地離開呢個國家……然後同我一齊埋咗佢……

TANG	Shut up! Sammy! Have you forgotten how she insulted you just now? Take the bat.
SAMMY	I don't want it! Let me go!
TANG	I swear, I will never treat you the way she treated me.
SAMMY	Please, let me go…
TANG	Don't be afraid. I'm on your side.
SAMMY	Let me go…
TANG	Why? You don't want to go back to Hong Kong, do you? You said you liked life here.
SAMMY	But I don't want a life with you. Don't you get it? I don't want to have anything to do with you. (*Pause.*) I don't even know you. (*Pause. Sammy backs up into a corner. Ling sadly sits in a corner.*)
TANG	It doesn't matter who I am. You have no choice because you know everything now. I'll bury either you or Ling. (*Tang suddenly hits Sammy over the head. Sammy touches the blood on her head in silence. She is stunned.*) Now you know I'm for real… (*Tang comes behind Sammy.*)… It won't be easy from now on. (*Tang holds up Sammy from behind, helps her with the wooden bat.*)

Don't fight this. You won't be faster than me. If you resist, you'll force me to make a decision. I hate making hasty decisions… We don't have to be in love, Sammy… We can have our own lives… We just have to live in this house and continue with the things that've been set up. (*He half pushes Sammy towards Ling.*)

First, you burn your passport… to prove you won't sneak out of the country. Then we bury her

連埋你D隨身物……跟住交換密碼同埋互相信任……所有嘢共同參予……責任就一齊承擔……唔係你想像中咁難……

【*Tang從後抱著Sammy，幫她握住木棍，慢慢放開Sammy*】

玲: 你一時意氣，我會原諒你。

【*Tang控制著自己不被動搖*】

TANG: ……舉起佢，扑落去。人同畜牲其實冇乜分別……

玲: ……我做所有嘢都係為咗你好……

TANG: ……記住，你係香港已經一無所有……

玲: ……我諗住屋企多個細路，就更加冇人懷疑……

TANG: ……冇人會怪你，大家都知你為咗生存……

玲: ……你以為真係咁容易，搵到一個愛你嘅人……

TANG: ……嚟啦，我哋重新開始。

together with your things. We do everything together so we're both responsible. Then we exchange passwords and trust each other. It's not as hard as you think… (*Tang slowly lets go of Sammy.*)

LING   You're acting on impulse. I'll forgive you. (*Tang controls himself. Lights change.*)

TANG   …There is no difference between people and animals…

LING   …Everything I did was for your own good…

TANG   …Don't look into her eyes…

LING   …I thought if we had a child, no one would suspect us…

TANG   …No one will blame you. We all know you did it to survive…

LING   …You think it's so easy to find someone you can love?…

TANG   …Please. I want to start all over.

尾聲

聖荷西一華人家庭的獨立大屋。

一切就像序幕一樣，只是比先前更靜，亦再沒有人站在窗前等待。

Tang從花園走進來，明顯剛作過園藝，他在屋內走動，時間慢慢流逝。

觀眾聽到遠處有汽車駛至、停下、再離去。

有人步至大門前，Tang看著大門被打開，玲提著一個粉紅色小皮箱進

玲： 冇……個墨西哥佬送返張詠兒個嗱上嚟……又係反方向上嚟，同一個路口錯兩次，蠢到死。

【*玲出花園，剩下Tang與皮箱*】

【*Tang將之打開，箱內全是嬰兒用品*】

【*燈漸暗*】

全劇完

EPILOGUE

The standalone home of a Chinese family in San José. Everything is the same as in the Prologue, only even quieter. Also, no one is standing at the window. Tang enters from the garden, apparently having just worked in the garden. He moves about in the house. Time passes. We hear a car approach from a distance. It stops, and then it leaves. Someone approaches the front door. Tang watches the door as it opens. Ling enters with a small pink suitcase

LING   He just returned Cheung Wing Yee's suitcase... He drove against traffic again. Made the same U-turn. Idiot.

(*Ling exits to the garden. Tang is left with the suitcase. Tang opens it. It's full of baby products.*)

(*Lights fade out.*)

THE END

The Hong Kong Arts Festival

The Hong Kong Arts Festival, first established in 1972, presents close to 150 performances and events by top international, regional, national and local talent during February and March each year. The eclectic mix of classical and contemporary works cater to an audience of about 120,000 including participants of the Festival's Young Friends Scheme. The Festival also commissions, produces and publishes new works independently or in collaboration with international partners. Festival information is available at www.hk.artsfestival.org.

香港藝術節簡介

香港藝術節成立於1972年，為國際藝壇重要的表演藝術節之一。多年來已邀請接近150個本地、亞洲及世界頂尖藝人及團隊到藝術節表演。藝術節的節目色色俱備，既顧及古典傳統口味，亦具備創意新奇和香港難得一見的表演形式，每屆入場觀眾人次達十二萬。近年，藝術節與亞洲區內其他藝術節積極合作，孕育新作，與國際上重要藝術機構聯合委約新創作，並支持不同領域的藝術家進行跨區跨媒體的合作。此外，香港藝術節「青少年之友」計畫，致力培養年青人對藝術的興趣，過去十八年間已有超過五十八萬個中學及大學生參與。經過三十八年的發展，今天的藝術節不論在表演藝人數目、演出水平、節目種類各方面，均為本地藝壇之最。

職員 Staff

行政總監 Executive Director
何嘉坤　　　　Tisa Ho

節目 Programme

節目總監 Programme Director
梁掌瑋　　　　Grace Lang
副節目總監 Associate Programme Director
蘇國雲　　　　So Kwok-wan
節目經理 Programme Manager
葉健鈴　　　　Linda Yip
外展經理 Outreach Manager
林慧茵　　　　Jess Lam
助理節目經理 Assistant Programme Manager
梁偉然　　　　Ian Leung
助理製作經理 Assistant Production Manager
蘇雪凌　　　　Shirley So
節目主任 Programme Officer
梁慧婷　　　　Leung Wai-ting

市場推廣 Marketing

市場總監 Marketing Director
鄭尚榮　　　　Katy Cheng
市場經理 Marketing Manager
周　怡　　　　Alexia Chow
助理市場經理 Assistant Marketing Managers
梁頌怡　　　　Kitty Leung
梁志勁　　　　Ruskin Leung
楊　璞　　　　Michelle Yeung

發展 Development

發展總監 Development Director
謝懷珠　　　　Joyce Tse
助理發展經理 Assistant Development Managers
陳艷馨　　　　Eunice Chan
蘇啟泰　　　　Alex So

會計 Accounts

會計經理 Accounting Manager
陳綺敏　　　　Katharine Chan
助理會計經理 Assistant Accounting Manager
曾愛明　　　　Ming Jung
會計文員 Accounts Clerk
黃國愛　　　　Bonia Wong

行政 Administration

行政秘書 Executive Secretary
吳鳳兒　　　　Vivian Ng
接待員／初級秘書
Receptionist / Junior Secretary
李美娟　　　　Virginia Li
辦公室助理 Office Assistant
鄭誠金　　　　Tony Cheng

職員（合約）Staff (contract)

節目 Programme

物流及接待經理 Logistics Manager
金學忠　　　　Elvis King
製作經理 Production Manager
廖卓良　　　　Liu Cheuk-leung
節目經理 Programme Manager
楊文秀　　　　Camelia Yeung
節目統籌 Programme Coordinator
汪文鈺　　　　Joy Wang
外展統籌 Outreach Coordinator
陳韻婷　　　　Alyson Chan
外展主任 Outreach Officer
蔡樂庭　　　　Vanessa Tsoi
節目及出版主任
Programme & Publications Officer
曾逸林　　　　Zeng Yilin
項目統籌 Project Coordinator
吳敦揚　　　　Dennis Ng
技術統籌 Technical Coordinators
陳寶愉　　　　Bobo Chan
陳詠杰　　　　Chan Wing-kit
陳佩儀　　　　Claudia Chan
關浩明　　　　Kan Kwan
蕭健邦　　　　Leo Siu
姚巧玉　　　　Tiffany Yiu

出版 Publication

編輯 Editors
戴佩珊　　　　Juliet Tai
魏家欣　　　　Luna Ngai
　　　　　　　Mikel Echevarría

市場推廣 Marketing

助理市場經理 Assistant Marketing Manager
陳惠芬　　　　Karrie Chan
助理市場經理（票務）
Assistant Marketing Manager (Ticketing)
梁彩雲　　　　Eppie Leung
票務主任 Ticketing Officer
關穎思　　　　Catherine Kwan
市場主任 Marketing Officer
范思雅　　　　Zia Fan
客戶服務主任
Customer Services Officers
陳肇輝　　　　Silvester Chan
黃萃婷　　　　Suki Huang
葉晉菁　　　　Jan Ip
黃伊衡　　　　Peri Asta Wong

行政 Administration

辦公室助理 Office Assistant
羅嘉輝　　　　Kevin Lo

督印人 Publisher	何嘉坤 Tisa Ho
主編 Editor	蘇國雲 So Kwok-wan
編輯審校 Executive Editor	梁偉然 Ian Leung
平面設計 排版 Designer	楚 翹 Devorah Jowie Chan
攝影 Photographer	張志偉 Cheung Chi-wai
協助 Coordinator	劉寶恩 Kitty Lau
出版 Published by	香港藝術節協會有限公司 Hong Kong Arts Festival Society Limited
印刷 Printer	雅聯印刷有限公司 Allion Printing Limited
版次 Edition	2011年3月第2版 2nd edition in March 2011
書號/ISBN	978-988-18176-9-3
定價/Price	港幣HK$100
版權垂詢: Copyright Enquiry	香港藝術節協會有限公司 Hong Kong Arts Festival Society Limited

香港灣仔港灣道二號12字樓
12/F, 2 Harbour Road, Wan Chai, Hong Kong
電話Tel: 2824 3555
傳真Fax: 2824 3798, 2824 3722
網頁Website: www.hk.artsfestival.org
電郵Email: afgen@hkaf.org